Fully Staffed

Fully Staffed

Linda A. Meredith

Dedicated
To the loving memory
Of my parents
Thomas & Elizabeth Meredith

Acknowledgements

This being my first attempt at writing, I am a little unsure as to where I start. So, I guess I ought to go right back to the beginning, to the two people who have always, and always will mean the world to me...

My wonderful parents Thomas & Elizabeth, I have so much to thank them for... They always encouraged my inquisitive mind, guided me along the way, kept me on the straight and narrow, and even survived my incessant talking! I send my love, and heartfelt thanks to these very special people. I know they're watching somewhere up above...

Thanks to my beautiful sister Christine, who taught me how to read and write amongst a lot of other things and made me appreciate the joy of reading. A perfect sister and mummy rolled into one, who always looked out for me, and still does! She's happy to give me a good listening to any time of day! I'm so proud to call her my sister. Love you Aggie!

Next, there are the men in my life. First, my wonderful husband Iain. Thanks for being so loving, supportive and reassuring even on the days I made it hard for you and wanted to dismember the keyboard AND throw the computer out of the window! Thank you for believing in me, I know you like a challenge! You can stop running now Puds. Guffs ya!

To my amazing sons, Terry & Christopher who always said I could do it- encouraged me to do it- and helped me do it! Thank you for having faith in me and giving me some very good material to work with! I am so proud to be your Mum, I love you with all my heart.

Reach for the crabs Terry, and Chris, thank you for bringing Spike into our lives, and reminding us how terrific it is to have a 'dag' in your life!

To my little sister Beverley – you are totally WICKED! Thanks to you and Michael for all your help, support and encouragement. We've had our share of laughter & tears, but the best thing we share, is our unique, loving relationship. Because I knew you...

Love and thanks to Nicky (Jonah) my sister-in-law and part time international dog rescuer, who has a lot to answer for, mainly our current, canine companions Louie & Tia. If there is a more selfless person in this world, I have yet to meet them!

Thank you to my in-laws Gordon & Joyce, for their unfailing encouragement, and for being my first 'read through'. I am grateful to both of you for everything you do.

All the staff, past and present at Oakham Veterinary Hospital, particularly David, Luke, Catriona and Chris – you guys are beyond amazing! Thank you for everything you did for Jake and Spike, and for all the kindness and compassion you showed us, in good times and bad.

Thanks to The Pet Blood Bank – what a remarkable, unique service you provide! Thank you for saving Spike's life! There must be thousands of pet owners all over the country who are immensely grateful to you, so on behalf of us all –THANK YOU!

I'd like to say a HUGE thank you to Debbie Poole, who was kind (brave) enough to take me on. A multi-talented, editorial genius, and a thoroughly nice lady, who expertly guided me through this unfamiliar process. I hope this is the beginning of a long friendship!

Finally, there is a very special person who quite simply, made this happen...

Brian L Porter - a brilliant, multi award winning author, who I am happy to say has become a very dear friend. It was after reading his books about the dogs he and his wife Juliet rescued, that led me to contact him. I am so very glad I did.

Brian's books about Sasha and Sheba, (who I fell totally in love with) amongst many others, motivated me into blowing the cobwebs off my keyboard and finish the labour of love I had started so many years ago. I believed writing about Jake would be cathartic, but it was far too painful back then...

Brian inspired me to finish the book, and has been there through every page and chapter, helping and encouraging. As you would expect from such a talented author, he is a very busy man, but he always finds the time to help and reassure.

He also told me he knew I could do it and helped me to believe in myself.

Brian, thank you for holding my hand and showing me the way. I will always be very grateful to you, Sasha and Sheba!

If you would like to know more about Brian and his work, visit his website at-

www.brianlporter.co.uk

Contents

PROLOGUE

It was very still and quiet in the tiny, airless room. The only sound breaking the silence was the rhythmic sound of the rain tapping down on the skylight window. It was a damp, chilly day - more like autumn than summer, but somehow, the weather reflected our demeanour that heart rending August day back in 1995. The 31st at nine thirty in the morning, to be precise - a day I will never forget.

If this was the right thing to do why did it feel so wrong? Why was it so painful? We had all done a lot of soul searching, and shed many, many tears over this devastating decision that could no longer be put off. We really had come to the end of the line; completely out of options, we simply didn't have a choice, but why, oh why did it have to end this way? In this unfamiliar, odd smelling room – it just wasn't right.

I lay beside him on the cold, red tiled floor, carefully lifted his head and wrapped both my arms around him; no one could hear my heart breaking.

It didn't take long…

Soon, his chest stopped rising, and I knew he had gone; slipped away to a better place; a place where once again, he would be a care-free puppy, with a fully loaded waggy tail, and no aches or pains. I just knew he would be reunited with my Mum & Dad, who would be waiting with open arms, ready to take him for the grand tour of his magnificent, new home. Alas, for those of us left behind, there was only pain, sorrow and an overwhelming feeling of sadness…

OUR GOLDEN BOY

Spike the Golden Labrador first came into our lives during the summer of 1980 and became an official member of our family in September.

At the time, we were living in Elgin, Scotland, as my husband Steve (being in the Royal Air Force) was posted to Lossimouth. Alan, a good friend of ours had a beautiful Labrador called Brandy, and she was expecting puppies! Although not planned, they were very welcome. Late July, Brandy produced five, gorgeous golden pups – they were absolutely beautiful! Ben, the sire, was also a Golden Labrador, so the puppies were off the scale in the cuteness department, we fell in love with them all! We went to visit them several times- sometimes, there would be one less as they found new homes.

Terry and Christopher (my sons) were totally smitten with these babies, and so desperate to have one, they weren't going to take 'no' for an answer. So, we harassed, bothered and stalked Steve every chance we got! Although Steve loved animals, he wasn't too keen on owning one, because of the life we led in the Air Force, however, with no prospects of an overseas posting on the horizon, I thought some pestering of the 'gentle persuasion type' might change his mind.

When there were only two left, we took the 'gentle' pestering to a different level! I even taught them the song 'Daddy wouldn't buy me a bow wow' and 'How much is that doggy in the window?' I hate to admit it, but I was almost as eager as the boys to have a pup, so, I played the 'Birthday Card' – as in Terry's 5th, which was only a few weeks away. Morning, noon and night he endured our 'singing' (for want of a better word!) till eventually, fearing for his sanity, he agreed!

Seemed like Daddy would be buying a 'bow wow' after all!

Unfortunately, by the time we told Alan of our decision, the two remaining pups had been diagnosed with Parvovirus, a very serious, viral disease.

The type Spike had was CVP2, which is highly infectious and potentially lethal if not diagnosed and treated quickly. Two of the pups that had been re-homed had already died, so the outlook was rather bleak. The pups were admitted into the vets for treatment, but the prognosis wasn't good, so we waited and prayed for a miracle.

They had been given nicknames by this time, Spit and Spike. Spit was the one that had been earmarked for us, and although the boys thought his name was cool, I couldn't wait to change it. Sadly, Spit died after a few days in the vets, and we were told to expect the worse for Spike. I couldn't tell the boys, I just kept praying for the miracle. Eventually, it came...

The vet called Spike his 'lucky pup' as he was on the brink of death, but somehow, with the medication, love and prayers, he managed to pull through. Luckily, there would be no need for any further medication and his prospects were looking good! I gratefully thanked St. Francis for answering my prayers.

As it was almost Terry's birthday, we thought it would be nice to wait and get him on the day. The boys were ecstatic! He was the most beautiful puppy I'd ever seen. He was very light in colour, much lighter than both his parents, he was almost cream. However, his velvety, soft ears were much darker, and had quite a pink nose too, so overall, he wasn't your 'bog-standard' looking Labrador. He was, quite simply, beautiful, and we couldn't wait to bring him home. When he arrived, he didn't take long to find his paws! He was in to everything – nothing was sacred, and no matter how we tried to teach the boys to remove precious items out of his reach, inevitably, they'd forget, and the dog would obliterate another toy!

He chewed anything and everything, but what was quite comical (although NOT at the time!) was the way he would chew one slipper belonging to Terry, and one slipper of Christopher's. Not content to have just one pair! Even their shoes weren't safe, it cost us a small fortune to keep replacing them!

He was also partial to their socks, and they too would disappear, like the shoes, one from each pair, however, for some reason, he tended to hide these in his bed. Like all puppies, his teeth were like razors, and the boys soon learned not to put their hands too close to his mouth! He gave them both a few good nips whilst they were playing, but, he never drew blood!

He followed me everywhere, which disappointed the boys, but I told them, if they fed him, and looked after him, maybe he'd follow them too – they weren't keen on that idea! Full of mischief, he fitted in well with Terry and Christopher; I really had my hands full! As the days passed, he became bigger and stronger, until he was bigger than his mum, who we saw when we visited Alan, or vice versa. He developed little traits, which both amused and frustrated us, but there was no way you could be mad at him.

He was very special, and always kept us entertained with his antics. He was never vicious or nasty, and he loved being with the boys. The only negative thing I can say about him, is that he was hard work to house train, so for a few months, my house smelled like a hospital, but we didn't' mind – we loved him - puddles and all!

He became quite well known around our estate, and unfortunately, it wasn't for his charm and charisma, it was due to the amount of times he managed to escape! He was like lightening! If you forgot to shut him in before answering the door, he'd sprint out between your legs! We all but put an electrified fence around the garden, but he still found a way out. Maybe we should have called him Houdini. Sometimes, I wouldn't even realise he'd gone, until there was a knock at the door.

On more than one occasion there was a phone call informing us that 'yer dag's on Lossie Road eatin' his way through the bins!' I was mortified, thinking people would think we weren't feeding him properly. I would go out and follow the trail of torn bin bags and scattered rubbish, and sure enough, he would be somewhere along the route! I spent a lot of time clearing up other peoples' rubbish thanks to Mr. Spike!

We soon established a routine, and very slowly, he became much better. He was very quick to learn, but he still insisted on peeing on the kitchen floor! I used to take him with me when I walked Terry to school, and when I collected him. It was so lovely to see Terry's face light up when he spotted Spike at the school gates.

There was one little incident that could have ended catastrophically but thankfully, it didn't. You know those times when things happen, and the very last thing you should do is laugh, but somehow, you just can't help yourself? The more you try not to, the harder it becomes. Well, it was a bit like that – hysteria almost took over in more ways than one! Only when the episode had ended, and I was relating the event to Steve, did I allow myself to laugh without feeling guilty.

One morning, just before Christmas, we were on our way to school, Terry was adamant that he wanted to hold Spike's lead. I tried to tell him that Spike was very strong, but you know what 5-year olds are like – they always know best! The school was just a ten-minute walk away, just over the main road, so I said Terry could hold him for a few minutes, just until we got near to the road, but he must hold the lead very tight and not let go. No sooner had the child taken hold of the lead, when Spike must have spotted something in the distance.

He took off at a great rate of knots, and Terry went with him. It had snowed the day before, and had dropped way below freezing during the night, so it was very, very slippery under-foot. Within seconds, Terry was flat out on his tummy sliding along behind Spike and holding onto the lead for all he was worth!

The road we were on sloped down to the main road at the bottom, so he slid quite easily. I ran after them shouting and screaming for Terry to let go, but no way was he releasing that lead, he went sailing down the road, holding on for dear life. It was quite difficult for me to run with a three- year- old Christopher in tow, but I did my best, I put him in his pushchair and belted down the road. The closer they got to the main road, the louder I shouted, but he refused to let go of that lead! He looked so funny, he went sliding past other kids, and even though I knew there was a busy road at the bottom, I couldn't stop smiling! What a terrible mother I must be!

Lord of all he surveys!

Only a few seconds stood between Terry and the main road. Thankfully, the Lollypop lady saw what was happening, and came to the rescue. She sprinted towards Terry, grabbed hold of him, and ambushed Spike with her lollypop stick, thus putting a swift, safe end to Spike's bid for freedom! Putting my arms around Terry, I expected him to be traumatised, but not at all. He was very, very proud of himself, because he hadn't let go of the lead! Spike seemed to be very pleased with himself too, but when I gave him 'the death stare' his ears went down, and his tail went between his legs; he knew he was in trouble. I didn't know whether to kill him there on the spot or take him home and do it in comfort!

I went into Terry's teacher and related the unfortunate incident. Then, boys in one hand – dog in the other, I made my way back home to change Terry and warm him up. Spike trotted along without a care in the world, tail wagging, and happy as you like, having completely forgotten about the mayhem he'd just caused a few moments ago. After a warm bath, some hot chocolate and dry clothes, Terry was ready to return to school, only this time, he asked if we could leave Spike at home. I was more than happy to comply with his request, and we agreed that in future, if the weather was bad, Spike would be stay at home!

AUF WEIDERSEIN SPIKE!

Just after Spike's first birthday in July '81, we were posted to Germany. Being in the Air Force, we were used to having to move, and Germany was a great opportunity - so we were all eager to go. Although we were quite pleased about the move, we were devastated to find out how much it would cost to quarantine Spike for six months on our return; We just didn't know what to do. Giving him to someone else was out of the question, but we simply couldn't afford the cost of quarantine. Even worse, none of us liked the thought of him spending six months in a quarantine kennel – we just couldn't do it.

Thankfully, my parents came to the rescue. They had met Spike on one of their visits and fallen under his spell! My dad, at the age of 70, had finally retired, so Spike would be a Godsend to them. He would give my Dad an interest and stop him from going 'stir crazy' and as my mum said, 'get him out from under her feet!' It was the best solution all round, and we knew 100% that he would be taken good care of, spoiled rotten in fact! Best of all, we wouldn't have to give him to strangers, he would be there when we visited, and when we returned, so everyone was happy. He soon settled in at my parent's home and had them whipped into shape with his routine in no time at all! He became my dads' shadow, which secretly, although Dad would say things like 'get away with you,' or 'get from under my feet' I knew he loved it. Mum used to tease him unmercifully. They loved him as much as we did, and he filled their lives with joy.

Spike proved to be a wonderful tonic for my Dad. No matter what the weather, dad would walk him morning, afternoon and evening, which was more than he got at my house! Their lives revolved around him, and I would imagine he loved it! Wherever they went, he went too. He was ruined, even to the point where he had his own sausages for his breakfast! No wonder he loved them, his paws were well and truly under the table! They were always playing with him, and one of the things he loved to play with was a balloon! My parents would play 'doggy in the middle' with him, and it was so funny to watch! The best bit for Spike, was killing it when he finally managed to catch it!

Smiley Spike

The boys and I stayed at my parents' house for a few weeks, before moving down to Steve's parents in Sussex where we would stay, until we had been allocated a married quarter at Laarbruch. We eventually flew out to Germany on October 5th, 10 weeks after Steve had gone.

The boys were beside themselves at the thought of going on an aeroplane - they were SO excited! Seeing their Dad again would be pretty good too!

We lived in a little village called Weeze (pronounced Veetsa) It was 4 km away from the base as Laarbruch, and a very popular place to live. We had a ground floor flat, right at the end of Stettiner Strasse, with fields surrounding three sides. It would have been ideal for Spike. At the back of the flats was an adventure playground for the boys – a quick hop over the balcony and they were there. Spike would have been in his glory with all those children to play with!

We had some wonderful neighbours opposite to us; Christine, Noel and their daughters Vivienne and Noelle, had recently arrived too. They also had their dog, Ben with them, which made me feel bad about leaving Spike...

Ben the little Dachshund, was absolutely adorable and like many a small dog, he feared nothing, and had the heart of a lion! He'd give any dog, any size a proper good verbal seeing too! Neither size nor decibels perturbed him. As far as Ben was concerned, he was the security guard for the entire block – all six flats belonged to him. Whenever any of the doorbells rang, Ben would bark – it was his gaff! Ben and the rest of his family became very special to us – they were extended family and helped us survive those three years without Spike...

We weren't completely 'animal-less' whilst we were there, we had three additions to our family – a budgie and two Boa Constrictors – Bessie & Billy. For goodness sakes!! I was fine with the budgie, who like thousands of budgies before him, had been called 'Joey' The lads called him 'Joey Vogel' - Vogel being the German for bird. The boys tried to teach it to talk, but Steve said it would have too much competition from their mum! Cheek! I couldn't help but tease them, by telling them that Joey only spoke German, therefore, they'd have to learn the language to speak to him. Naughty Mummy!

The Snakes were a different kettle of fish! I wasn't afraid of them – I didn't particularly dislike them, but there was no way I was getting involved with them! Steve had built a Vivarium for them, but I was still a little sceptical where the boys were concerned. They were told never, EVER to even think about opening the cage. Using the 'mum's not messing' stare always helped to get a point across! They were very good, all things considered, but we did have a constant stream of kids coming to see them! If I'd charged them, I'd be a wealthy woman now! The boys became very popular at school, especially when Steve took their discarded skins in to 'show and tell!'

The time seemed to fly in Weeze, but we did manage to visit both sets of parents a few times. Steve's Mum and Dad came to stay with us too, but sadly, my parents wouldn't come out – they wouldn't leave Spike – which made me feel very guilty. But, when we did get to see my parents, we found both parents and dog, very happy. Seeing how contented they were had convinced us that we had indeed made the right decision. Spike was Daddy's boy. Talk about one man and his dog!

By the summer of 1984, our three-year stint in Germany was coming to an end. Steve was told that our new posting was to be in the East Midlands – Rutland to be precise. This was only a couple of hours drive away from my parents, and about forty minutes away from Steve's brother Brian, his wife Plum – (because she's so tiny) and their daughters Melanie and Emma. Brian was also in the Air Force and was stationed just down the road from where we would be. Their house was on the outskirts of Peterborough, it would be great having them so close – we would get to see them more often. The kids would get to reacquaint themselves with their cousins, and their doggy, Dougal – also a beautiful Labrador. However, our first priority would be to get Spike home.

It was sad to say goodbye to our wonderful friends, they were going to be living in Wiltshire, at R.A.F. Lynham, and though we promised to keep in touch, we knew we would never be this close again. With a heavy heart, we packed our belongings, Kids, Snakes and the Vogel, and headed back to Blighty and our families.

We were lucky enough to be given a nice, three-bedroom house, and immediately got to work to make it a home. Within hours – literally three hours of arriving, I had been to the medical centre twice! The first time with Chris, as he fell over and cut his head, and arrived back home to find Terry had fallen off a ladder and hurt his arm. I just couldn't believe it!!

When the Medical Officer saw me back again within the hour, he said 'I see your boys intend to keep me busy!' Kids!! Thankfully, there were no broken bones, and nothing that hugs, kisses and sweets couldn't put right.

As soon as we had unpacked, and sorted out boxes etc., we set off up the A1 to get Mr. Wigs. However, once we arrived, things seemed to be a little strained. We were eager to get our boy back, but mum and dad were reluctant to part with him. I completely understood why, it was just something I hadn't considered, and it was so hard to accept. This was going to take some significant thought; it would be a massive decision – one that we could not make lightly.

We just had to be sure to do what was right – it might not be what we all wanted, but life treats us all that way sometimes, and you simply must do what is right. We lost sleep and stressed about it, but in the end, we did what we considered to be right, and that was to leave him with my parents. It was a hard decision, but in the end, knowing how resilient kids are, we knew the boys would soon get over the fact he was staying with Grandad. To take him away, well, it would have broken my Dad's heart, and THAT simply wasn't an option.

The boys were bitterly disappointed with our choice – not for the first (or last) time we were the worst parents in the world! I explained to them that Spike was happy living with their Grandparents, after all, he'd been there for three years, and spent only one with us, so for him, his home was with them. Trying to convince the boys of that this was the right thing to do was not easy, but in the end, they agreed, and when they realised we would only be a two-hour drive away, they were fine.

We soon settled in to life in the Midlands – the boys started school, and life was ticking along nicely. Christmas was a coming, and this year, we were having my parents down to stay. We were all looking forward to seeing them and wondered what Spike would make of Bessie & Billy; Short work if I had to put money on it! I drove up to collect them a few days before Christmas. Spike was always up for a ride in the car and was the first in!

Once we got to the house, he was beside himself, not knowing where to strike first! Terry and Chris won, as he set to, and covered them both with Spikey kisses! The Christmas Tree went for a ball of chalk, as did my little crib on the hearth. With one swish of Spike's tail, Baby Jesus, the donkey and one of the Kings, were unceremoniously evicted several feet on to the carpet - you just had to laugh!

Thankfully, there was no permanent damage to the figures or the tree, and everything was soon back in place. Spike was beside himself when he spotted the balloons the boys had put up, and wore himself, and his bark out trying to kill them. It didn't take long for him to make our house his own. After he'd peed all around the garden (front and back) and sniffed out every room, he was ready to settle down. He was now four and a half years old, but still behaved like an overgrown puppy, and a delightful one at that! He had decided that the accommodation on offer would suit his needs perfectly, until it was time for him to go home!

On Christmas day, he had his own Christmas presents (all edible) to open, which he did with great enthusiasm; he just loved a present. At lunch time, he had more or less the same Christmas Dinner as we did, but I drew the line at giving him sprouts, and eating at the table with us (as my youngest suggested!) We had so much fun with him, but as the saying goes, time passes quickly when you're having fun – and believe me, it certainly did. All too soon, it was time to take Mum, Dad and Spike back home. We had a huge Audi 100 at the time, so there was plenty of room for everyone. Spike jumped straight onto the front seat, but Dad was having none of it, so he settled down in the foot well. It wasn't long before he was almost on the seat with Dad. Thank goodness, the roads weren't that busy back in 1984!

We stayed in Stalybridge to celebrate the New Year with my parents and the rest of the family. Little did we know when we wished everyone a Happy New Year, it destined not to be. 1985 would turn the lives of my little family upside down and would bring no happiness for Steve's family or mine...

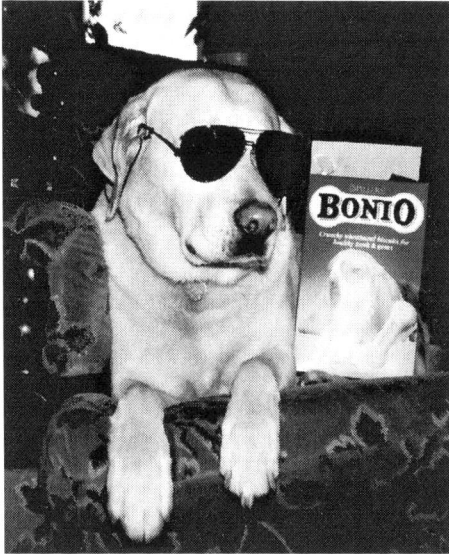

Wiggy Cool!

ANNUS HORRIBILIS
(with bells on!)

I always feel optimistic at the start of a New Year, wondering what lies ahead for us, but only a few days in, we received some devastating news. Brian had been seriously injured in an accident whilst travelling home from work. He was on his motorbike, when a car hit him at some speed, and had been taken to the hospital at Peterborough. However, such was the nature of his injuries; we just didn't know if he'd pull through. It hit us so hard it hurt - We were absolutely shattered. Steve and his parents were inconsolable, God only knew what Plum and the girls were going through, my heart broke for them all. Steve didn't know what to do with himself he was overwhelmed with sorrow. I tried my best to comfort him, but it was very, very hard.

I knew how much he loved his brother, he'd always admired and looked up to him, but it's the kind of thing that men don't' talk about – especially brothers, and the thought that he might never get to tell his big brother how much he meant to him, was tormenting him.
 We all fervently prayed for his recovery, but there wasn't much in the way of good news. Each time the phone rang, we were afraid to answer it – afraid of what it might tell us. Finally, after what seemed to be forever, we knew he was going to be okay, and that was all that

mattered! We allowed ourselves a little optimism, and breathed a huge sigh of relief, but we weren't out of the woods yet.

Sadly, after many, many months in hospital, the doctors informed Brian that he needed to have his right arm and leg amputated. After months of trying, there was no way they could save them. Steve took this news very badly, as did his parents, but Plum and the girls were incredibly strong and supportive, we all tried to follow their example, and be strong for them! Brian was quite remarkable throughout all this. I admire his tenacity – whatever it was he was feeling, he went to great lengths to make sure none of us would know. He's quite an amazing guy.

A couple of weeks after Brian's accident my Mum had a stroke, which ultimately, resulted in the loss of mobility, although she retained her speech. Psychologically, the inability to communicate as well as she had done, would do far more damage to her than being able to walk without assistance. Even though she could still talk, her poor old brain had taken a bit of a battering, subsequently causing memory loss and confusion. On the outside, we tried to see the lighter side of things, and, in her more lucid moments, laughed and joked about some of the things she would say. However, inside our hearts were breaking to see such an independent lady reduced to being totally reliant on others – something she would have absolutely hated!

My poor old Dad was shattered, visiting the hospital twice a day to give my Mother a good listening to, but he stuck with it. Then there was Spike to walk in between times. Not that he didn't want to see Mum, he was just tired out, bless him. Fortunately, the hospital was just a few minutes' walk away at the end of the road they lived on, so it was easy enough for him to get there. Having Spike also meant that Dad had a 'Get out of jail free card' so when he'd had enough, he'd say he had to leave, as 'little lad will be waiting for me!'

We took turns at visiting the patients - one weekend to Brian, the next, to my Mum and work/school in between. It was quite exhausting, but our exhaustion was nothing compared to what our loved ones were going through. After a few weeks of this schedule, my dad said he was feeling the pressure, and was feeling unwell and tired all the time. He then went on to suggest it might be a good idea to take Spike home to live with us. That's when I began to suspect that there was a little more than stress and tiredness troubling him. Sadly, I was right...

At the end of March, after endless nagging by all his kids to go to the doctors, my lovely, old Dad, was diagnosed with cancer and admitted to hospital there and then. I, like the rest of my siblings, was distraught. They told us to prepare for the worst, and to think in weeks rather than months! Knowing my Dad, I was optimistic that he would stay longer – just to prove them wrong. He could be quite tetchy when it came to people telling him what to do! He went into a different hospital on the other side of Manchester, which made it an absolute nightmare visiting them both. The worse bit was, how were we going to explain all this to Mum?

When Dad had asked me to take Spike back, I knew there had to be something seriously wrong. Wild horses couldn't have torn him apart from his lad. I spoke to Christine, my other sister about this. Like me, she knew how much Spike meant to our Dad, and if he was asking me to take him away, then there must be something he wasn't telling us.

I hadn't seen much of Christine for several years, with being in Scotland and then Germany, so it was wonderful to be by her side again. She had always looked out for me when I was young, and always had a hug on standby! Very reluctantly, I took Spike home with me, hoping against hope, that it would only be a temporary measure, and he would soon be back with Dad.

My visits to Stalybridge were every weekend now, I wanted to see my dad as often as I possibly could. Steve visited Brian on week nights, and we discussed the patients every Sunday night when I arrived home. There simply didn't seem to be enough days in the week, let alone hours in the day. My poor boys, bless them, got used to seeing the back of their parents, but having Spike around went some way to make up for it.

After a few weeks, my Dad was allowed home, and went to live with my eldest sister, which meant that I could take Spike to see him whenever I visited. One hot, Saturday afternoon in June, we arrived as usual at lunchtime, and Spike immediately took up his position at my dad's side. Dad was very poorly by now, but still managed to rub his lad's ears. Normally, after receiving his ear rub, Spike would disappear off and wander around the house, to see if there was anyone else around who might want to make a fuss of him.

However, this day, he stayed right beside my dad; he made no attempt to go anywhere. As we were leaving that day, I felt the need to hold my dad a little longer. I will never forget the sadness I felt as I watched my father hug Spike as we were leaving. Usually, he would only tolerate a hug for a minute or two, but this hug was different – it seemed to last a long time. Somehow, it was almost as if they knew that this hug would be their last…

Sadly, our wonderful Dad passed away the following day, in the early hours of Sunday morning, June 30th.

I was at my brother's house when the call came, and we immediately rushed to our other sister's where Dad was staying. When we went in, Spike ran straight upstairs to dad's room, only to be shooed away. It didn't deter him – he came and put his head on my knee, and as I leaned over to hug him, he licked my tears. He knew our wonderful Daddy had gone. ……. Thankfully, Christine arrived soon after, so we were able to console each other, but as always, she comforted her little sister. My second Mum, she means the world to me. I couldn't wish for a better big sister – even though I tease her unmercifully about her name.

My parents believed in naming their offspring after members of their family. My mum was the eldest of 13, my Dad, the second of 4, so this gave them plenty of scope! Poor Christine ended up being called after both of our grandmothers, and Christine, I guess they just liked the name. So officially, she is Agnes, Mary, Christine – and I don't plan on letting her forget it! Love you Aggie!

The next few weeks were filled with sadness and tears. Seeing my poor Mum in such anguish only added to my heartache. She was still in hospital because of the stroke, but now with Dad gone; she felt she had nothing to go home to.

Back home, I was finding it difficult to function, but thankfully, having Spike around seemed to make it more bearable. The boys were amazing during that time, in their own little way, they tried to help by being extra, especially good, and it didn't go unnoticed.

Spike was very well behaved too; Dad had had much more time to spend training him, and he was a credit to him. He was still as daft as a brush though! He was happy enough to fetch a shoe but wouldn't bring two that matched. He would fetch shoes all day, but no way would he bring a pair. Maybe something to do with his time in Scotland? He soon stamped his paw mark on our house and marked out his territory. He must have peed on every tree trunk and blade of grass on the camp during his first trip out for a walk!

He was such a joy, you couldn't help but laugh at him, and he truly helped to ease my pain and get through those first few months without Dad. Somehow, I felt that Dad was still close to me, apart from being Daddy's girl, our mutual love for Spike bound us eternally together. Although the boys were happy at the prospect of Spike staying with us permanently, they were sad about the loss of their Granddad.

It was at this time, that his list of names expanded. I've no recollection as to why he became Wiggy, Mr. Wigs, or Wiglet, but he responded to them all!

Although we had a back garden, it wasn't very big, and was separated from the one's either side by a wire fence. Our neighbours on one – Daphne & Colin, had two lovely dogs; a Bearded Collie, and a Westie, both of which were adorable. I'd gotten to know them quite well since we'd moved in. However, for some reason, when Spike arrived, he took umbrage to the little Westie - it was like a red rag to a bull whenever he saw him, and he developed one of his naughtier habits. Whenever the Westie appeared by the fence, Spike would go over to it – cock his leg – and pee through the fence – all over it! I was horrified and dreaded the day that either Daphne or Colin mentioned the fact that their dog was always wet when it came in! Only many years after did I tell Daphne what my naughty dog had done!

Whenever anyone came to the door, no matter what for, Spike would immediately run to find a present for him or her. He appeared with various items; stuffed toys, shoes, his dinner bowl, the head from the hoover, in fact anything he could lay his chops on! Don't try to take it from him though – only when he was ready to part with it would he leave go!

Another thing Spike took umbrage to, were the gates at the camp entrance. They were like the kind you see at level crossings – with the dangly bits. He would walk past them, and give them a wide berth, but, should they be raised or lowered whilst he was in close proximity, there would be mayhem! He would try his best to destroy them and held onto them by his teeth like something possessed! Maybe when they moved, they emanated some kind of high pitch noise that distressed him? We never did find out, but whatever it was, he saw those gates as the enemy, and as such, they must be destroyed! He brightened up the guard duty many a time!

One summer night, Spike's escapades almost got Steve a thump on the nose! Steve always took Spike for a quick walk last thing at night, just around the block for his last 'sniff' of the day. This particular night, they came back around the edge of a huge, empty field, surrounded by a hawthorn hedge. The MOD had decided to turn this field into a BMX track for the kids. Spike ran ahead, as usual, but disappeared through a hole in the fence into the field. He didn't come back when he was called, but as Steve got closer to the hole in the fence, he could hear Spike barking. Not only could he hear barking, he could also hear a voice, in a rather loud whisper. Curious, he crouched down, and went through the fence. It was pitch black, and he couldn't really see anything, so he shouted for Spike again.

He heard him bark and headed toward the direction of the sound. To his horror, a rather large man appeared in front of him, demanding that Steve keep his dog under control, or else etc. etc., Then, he heard someone giggling, and turned to see a young lady sitting on the floor with Spike. He now realised what was happening!

The 'courting couple' were getting a 'little friendly' when Spike appeared, and finding them on the floor, he must have thought that they were playing, and decided he wanted to join in! Steve was now close enough to see that the pair of them in a state of undress. He quickly put Spike on his lead, apologised to the couple, and sped off home. When he told me about it, he couldn't keep his face straight, and said he didn't know who was more embarrassed, them or him! I definitely know who it wasn't!

An extra treat that 1985 had in store for us, was a fire at our house! I happened to be in the medical centre when the alarm went off. The announcement said " FIRE FIRE FIRE – fire at … then went on to say my address!! I froze, The medics ran down the corridor, and I ran after them. When they asked what I was doing, I told them it was my house, and my boys were there!!! I was beyond fear!!! The boys were on school holiday, and Steve was home too, being on the night shift. Oh my God, it must be bad if Steve's called the fire brigade!!!!

I jumped into a little RAF mini with one of them, and sped off to my house, just a few minutes' drive away. It was during the time of the fireman's strike, so the 'Green Goddesses' were out in force. When we turned the corner, I could see one outside my house. The medic gave me strict instructions to stay in the car. Yeah, right, I was really (not) going to do that!!

It appeared to be very quiet at the house – not a sign of anyone. All I could see, was a hose stretching from the big, green engine to the house – no boys, no Steve, no Wigs! In that split second, when your brain tries to process what it's seeing, and comparing it with what you want it to see, I'd convinced myself they were all injured. There was an ambulance parked in front of the fire engine, they must all be in there…

Then, all of a sudden, just like on the television when the smoke clears, and the hero appears, Mr. Wigs came out from the back garden, a huge, fluffy stuffed owl that the boys let him play with, bulging out of his mouth. I threw myself on him and hugged him sooo tight! Next, Steve appeared, covered with black smoke and two white eyes. "the boys are fine, they're in the front of the fire engine" he told me.

I cannot find any words that could express how relieved and thankful I was, knowing everyone was safe. I rushed to hug my boys, my world, and thanked the good Lord above for keeping them all safe. While this was going on, Mr. Wigs was entertaining the firemen, rolling on his back to have his tummy rubbed, offering his paws, and letting them think he was going to let them have his minging owl.! Had it not been for Mr. Wigs making me laugh, I may have gone a wee bit crazy that day, especially when I discovered the cause of the fire...

Like all other parents, we invested a lot of time instilling rules into our boys. And, like the majority of kids, they always know best, and cannot wait to bestow the benefit of their wisdom upon us. Once a 'do not' has been implanted within the grey matter, they perceive it as a challenge if deemed as inapplicable to them (I'm old enough/clever enough/that's for babies' stuff) and just can't wait to try it out - and try it out they did!

Never, ever touch the cooker/fire etc., being at the top of the list. Being grounded until you are thirty being one of the punishments on offer. But as soon as I'd left for work, after already having eaten breakfast that day, they decided to have some toast. Not possessing a toaster in those days, we used the grill which was knee high, as opposed to eye level. Being electric, it took a while to heat up, and having run right out of patience, they left it and went to watch t.v. They also left the bread there. It wasn't long before there was a lot of smoke and big BANG!

Steve must have thought he was in the middle of a living nightmare when the boys woke him up! Can you imagine the dulcet tones of the offspring "you need to get up Dad, the house is on fire "They in turn, must have been equally worried once they found out that I was on my way home! I can look back and smile about it now: Especially, as they've admitted now they're all grown up, they were more scared of me coming home than any damage the fire could have done! I have no idea what they're talking about – bad babies! It's one of those incidents that you embarrass them with when they bring a new girlfriend home!

NEW HORIZONS?

Sadly, four years later, Steve and I went our separate ways, which also meant that we had to move out of our home on the base. This is standard procedure within the military, (it was in those days) The husband had to move into single accommodation on the base, and the wives could stay in the house. You were then given sixty days to sort out your differences, after that, if there was no resolution, the M.O.D. would issue an eviction notice. Not as harsh as it sounds – you couldn't be rehomed by the local council without a notice of eviction, and this usually took several months.

Because the boys were at school, and I had a full-time job, we were able to stay in the area, and I was given a house in the nearby village. Sadly, there was one member of our little family who didn't make it to the village. Joey Vogel had left us for the big aviary in the sky, not long after the fire. We had had a little ceremony in the back garden and buried him in a quiet little corner. Complete with a cross made from two lollipop sticks!

Had I not had the boys, or full-time job, I would have been sent back to Stalybridge. At first, it seemed strange living in a neighbours community rather than an RAF base, but we soon adjusted to 'civvie' life!

Steve remained on the base for a couple of years, with his snakes, until he was posted to Belize, on the east coast of Central America: a posting that he eagerly accepted! Not only was he able to have his snakes, he kept crocodiles too! He had lived in Singapore with his parents as a teenager (his father was also in the R.A.F.) and he just loved the heat. It was a new beginning for him too, and he was happy doing something he had previously, only ever dreamed about doing. He also remarried, but we remained friends and kept in touch, until his untimely death in 2007. A very sad day, one which the boys and I will never forget. He was only 55…

Back in the village, before any of that happened, I met a wonderful man called Iain, (who was also in the RAF) and things were going well. I had seen him around for some time, but it was quite a while before he became my 'boyfriend' The boys seemed to approve, and so did The Wigs, very important to have his vote! It was only a matter of time before he moved in, and very soon, he popped the question! He sent a beautiful bouquet of flowers to work for me, with a card that read "Now you're free and single, would you like to change your name?" Well, I wasn't going to let an opportunity for a wind-up pass by!

He popped into the shop where I worked at lunch time, and I showed him my flowers. He had a huge smile on his face as he asked (tongue in cheek) who they were from.

"well, that's just it" I said – trying not to make eye contact.

"I have no idea – there was no card with them. Maybe it fell off in the van, or I've got a secret admirer!"

His smile disappeared, and I had to bite my lip to stop laughing. If he wanted to marry us (me, the lads & the Wigs) he was jolly well going to ask me! By the time I'd finished work, he was at the door waiting for me, and as soon as I saw him, I burst out laughing, and sang like a Canary!

Later that evening, Iain took us all out for dinner, and I guess, to repay my earlier wind-up, he got down on one knee, in front of every-one in the pub and asked me to marry him – the boys were beyond mortified! He said he wasn't moving till I gave him an answer – I could feel myself blushing, at my age, I didn't know where to look. I asked him to let me think about it, but he stayed on the floor. So, I said "Oh go on then, if I've nothing better to do that day, I'll marry you: can we have some pudding now!"

It was St. Georges day, so the boys couldn't resist the odd pun about dragons! Cheeky babies!

The following day, Iain said he had a surprise for us. He thought it would be nice if we had a little break, and had just the thing in mind, that he was sure the boys would love...

SLOW BOAT TO ABINGDON

It was May when we put Iain's idea into action. Terry was almost 15, Chris 12 and the First Admiral of The Barge was 10. We made some wonderful, happy memories on that holiday...

Admiral Wigs!

The base where Iain was stationed owned a narrow boat, which they rented out, and discounts were given to serving personnel, even more so if you worked at that base. We mentioned it to the boys, who were well up for a trip on a boat, and like us, thought it would be a great adventure. Luckily, they allowed animals on board, which was the icing on the cake. We had no idea how Spike would react to the canal, but we knew he was a good little swimmer, mad for water, so we weren't overly concerned about him falling in. In fact, knowing his love of the water, we thought about having a sweepstake to see how many times he would be overboard during the trip!

The boat was moored at Blisworth Marina in Northamptonshire, by the Grand Union Canal. As Iain was getting instructions on how to handle the boat, the boys and I unpacked our supplies, and sorted out sleeping arrangements. It was a huge 56-foot boat, designed to take eight people, so there was plenty of room for us four (5).

The sun was shining, the sky was brilliantly blue, and we just couldn't wait to get going!

Eventually, Iain came aboard, and we were ready for the off! There were some maps lying around which showed interesting places to visit, good food etc. It was all very exciting. We'd decided to head for Abingdon, as the boys and I lived there when they were little. It was also a beautiful place. Iain, the boys and Mr. Wigs were at the helm, and I was making a cup of tea. The boys had chosen names for us – they were Admirals, Captain Pud (Iain) Galley Slave (me) and First Admiral (of The Barge) that'll be Mr. Wigs!

An hour or so into our journey, we came upon our first obstacle – The Braunstone Tunnel. We'd seen it on the map but had no idea how very narrow the tunnel was – barely enough room to pass another boat, and only then by scraping alongside it! This tunnel was 1.87kl long, 4.8 metres wide, and 3.76 high. It was pitch black inside once we were right inside, with every sound ricocheting around the walls; a bit scary really. Having never been on a narrowboat before, I thought we were being a little adventurous going through this tunnel.

I was sat on one of the bunks at the back, just beneath the steps down into the cabin, and I could see nothing. Suddenly, there was this huge thud beside me. I jumped out of my skin and screamed at which point, Spike began to bark. He was the thud - obviously afraid too, as he'd hurled himself onto me, and when I screamed – he barked! The lads thought this was highly amusing, which, only when we were safely out of the tunnel did Spike and I breathe again!

Where's the Admiral's hat?

Spike was quite happy on the boat, and contrary to our suspicions of his jumping overboard at every chance he got, he kept all four paws dry! I soon noticed that our days were planned around pubs! The maps showed every single pub en-route, most of them selling food, and Iain said, seeing as how we were on holiday, he didn't think it fair that I was cooking every day.

Really? It wouldn't be anything to do with sampling all the different beers at each pub, now would it? Our days went from The Red Lion to The Dog and Pheasant., and any other pubs in between! Iain was in his element drifting from one pub to the next, and Spike was just happy to be with us, but insisted on barking at all the animals in the fields as we passed them, and any other dogs that had the cheek to be walking along his towpath near his boat!

We had a glorious week, but unfortunately, never made it to Abingdon. Half-way through the week, we arrived at Banbury, famous for its 'Ride a Cock Horse' nursery rhyme. As the crow flies, it's around forty-five miles from Abingdon, so we decided to stop for lunch, so

Iain and Spike went off in search of a pub! It was during lunch that we realised, if it had taken us two and a half days to get to Banbury, then it would surely take us the same length of time to get back, and we only had a week! We had failed to consider the number of hours we'd lose due to the water shortage.

Because of this, the locks were locked every night at six, so wherever you were, you had to stay. This lost many hours for everyone. I'm sure you could make it there and back in a week under normal circumstances, but not this week! Spike couldn't have cared less either way – he was enjoying his breakfast sausages, extra fussing and all the new doggy smells!

We managed to make it to the end of the week without a soggy doggy, that is, until we were almost back to the marina. We came upon the dreaded Braunstone Tunnel, and had to join the queue to go through. We were all chatting about what a lovely time we'd had, and how much Spike had kept us amused. Just watching the world go by, I noticed a lollypop stick floating past. The next thing I heard was splash – dog overboard!

Because we were around other boats, we'd put Spike's lead on, and secured it to the front of the boat, so we had no time to think, we needed to get him free – and quick! While Iain, Terry and I jumped onto the bank and tried to take his weight, Chris set about undoing the lead. Thankfully, it took only a few minutes to release him, but it seemed much longer. We threw a towel around him and gave him a good rub down. We had managed a whole week without a soggy doggy. Seen lots of other animals, ducks, birds etc., but that lollypop stick just sent him over the edge. Literally. It was a stick too far!

He was none the worse for his ordeal, but boy, did he stink, and lucky for us, we would have to spend at least an hour in a warm car with him on the way home. Oh joy – Eau du Stinkee Poochy!

We all agreed, that trip was one of the happiest times we spent together as a family – it always will be.

All to soon the beautiful summer gave way to autumn, and before we knew it, Christmas has landed. Iain and I had sort of talked about getting married in April, which would be a year after our engagement, but we thought we'd get Christmas out of the way before making any plans. Unbeknown to us, events were taking place in another country that would scupper our plans of an April wedding...

HERE COMES THE (WAR) BRIDE!

January is always seems to be a busy month for us, starting with Christopher's birthday. This year, he would be become a teenager. As if I didn't have enough problems!

We had planned to take him bowling, followed by a stop off at one of his favourite eateries, but when Iain came home from work, one look at his face told me there was something wrong. Very wrong. It was the beginning of the war in Iraq, and the entire station had been put on 48 hour standby to fly out. We all looked to each other, not knowing what to say. We did however, make sure that nothing was going to ruin Chris's birthday, so we set off to the bowling alley, and tried to forget, if only for a little while, what the implications of a war with Iraq would mean.

Back home, we had a video (remember those!) for the boys to watch, so we popped up to the families' club for a little snifter, but both felt we could do with one in view of the news, which everyone was talking about. One of our friends pointed out something which neither of us had thought about. Unfortunately, being unmarried, if anything should happen to Iain in Iraq, there would be no provision for me and the boys – no help whatsoever.

Now Iain, being the caring chap, he is, wanted to ensure, that should the worst happen, we would be taken care of. With this in mind (and a couple of alcoholic beverages in our tummies) we decided that first thing in the morning, we would pay a visit to our local registrar, to see if anything could be done. They were amazing when we told them of our plight and as a result they granted us a special license! We were married exactly one week after 19/1/91 a palindrome, thought to be lucky by some, (though there are times when I would disagree!) A little spooky too, because of the fact there was no special planning for this wedding, but the numbers one and nine are our respective birthdays too, so we couldn't have chosen a more appropriate date. I took it as a good omen, and means that yours truly, is officially a war bride!

The day was bright and sunny, but bitterly cold. The family showed up en masse, so our little house was like Piccadilly Circus – circus being the operative word! As for Spike, well, he was just beside himself in the midst of the mad-house, and his tail was at warp speed wag all day. It's a wonder his tummy wasn't rubbed away by the end of the day. If I could have taken him with me to the registry office- I would!

The day passed in a whirl of happiness, cuddles and lots of laughter. Our evening reception was in the Families Club on the base, and we threw the doors open to anyone who wanted to come. After all, this could be the last time for a knees-up…

Thankfully, none of the people we knew were called up to go, and things slowly got back to normal – well, as normal as they can be in our house! I did consider asking for a refund seeing as how Iain didn't' go…

One of the things I *hadn't* done since moving to the village, was getting Spike's nametag updated. I kept meaning to do it, but always forgot, so Iain said he'd make a new one at work.

We needed to make sure that if he ever tried to go back to the house on camp, he would be brought back. Spike loved the large garden, which was decidedly bigger than the one we had on camp, and happily spent most of his time out there – if the weather was good! He had met the beautiful Labrador next door when we first moved in, but eighteen months later, his ardour was unyielding! Cindy and her family were lovely, and had been so welcoming when we first arrived in the village.

Sometimes, Spike was like a lovesick pup, and would cry through the fence to her. They became really good friends. I'm sure he would have had me buy flowers and chocolates for her if he could!

However, there was the odd occasion, when Spike just had to go with his instincts, and take off! Not being able to get to Cindy through the fence, he tried to go around, but never quite managed to get in their garden. He had never, ever run away from either my parents or us (apart from his expeditions in Scotland) but a doggy's needs sometimes just, must be attended to, and I think Cindy awakened Spikes! He appeared to revert to his puppy days - he seemed to have extra 'wag' in his tail too!

We bought fencing etc., and doggy proofed the garden as best we could, but there was one bit we missed – and he found it! Right at the bottom of the garden, a hedge separates us from another house. We hadn't bothered to fence over this, as it seemed impenetrable. Wrong! We had not realised how strong a doggy's urges could be! After one of his disappearing acts, we watched to see how he got out. He sauntered down towards the boundary hedge, and after a quick look around, thrust himself through it! He then casually strolled down their path and ran like hell when he got to their gate! There were no flies on Mr. Spike!

One of his antics that still make me smile involves him going walk-about, though at the time, it wasn't funny at all. We were decorating the bedrooms. I was doing the painting, and I'd left the conservatory doors open so that Spike could go out if he wanted to. Just when I was up to my armpits in paint (yes, I am seriously that messy!) the phone rang. Cursing under my breath, I looked for something to wipe my hands on, and then answered the phone.

'Hello' I said.

'Hello there' the caller then identified herself as living at one of the more prestigious houses in the village – more like an estate than a home, where landed gentry had once lived. What could she want with me?

'Do you have a dog called Spik?' she asked.

'Pardon me' I replied, 'what did you say?'

'Do you have a dog called Spik?' she repeated.

What was she on about- Spik? Then the penny dropped.

'Oh, do you mean Spike? Oh yes, I have a Golden Labrador, but his name's Spike, why do you ask?'

'Because my dear, he's up here frolicking with my girls!'

'No, I don't think so, it can't be my Spike, he's in the garden, or at least that's where he should be.' Then, a little teensy-weensy doubt crept into my mind.

'Hold on a minute I'll go and check'.

I went down into the garden and called for him. He was nowhere to be seen. Even the promise of a chewy didn't work. Oh dear, he'll be frolicking alright when I got my hands on him! I went back to the phone, apologised profusely to the lady on the other end of the line and told her that I was leaving immediately to collect him. She went on to say, that she had shut him in an outside shed, but he was whimpering. I just bet he was!

I got in the car, not because the house was any distance, but because I was covered in paint, very scruffy, and really didn't have time for a shower. It would also be easier to throw him in the car and beat a quick retreat! As I drove up the driveway, I began to feel rather laughable with my paint-covered clothes, streaked hair to match and 'frolicking' dog. I needn't have worried, as she said she found it 'rather amusing' and didn't realise she had an extra dog until he stared barking! It was obviously his northern accent she didn't recognise!

I opened the car door as she opened the shed, and out he came, head down, tail between the legs. He looked neither left nor right but walked straight to the car and jumped into the back seat. He knew he was in trouble. I thanked the lady of the manor, apologised once more, and drove off back down the driveway.

Once home, the procedure was repeated in reverse. Open car door – dog alights – straight into house – not looking left or right, but straight in to his bed. I scolded him a little bit as I removed his collar. 'What are you like? Fraternising with those fancy bitches, they're out of your league boy'. At this, he just wagged the very tip of his tail, something he only did when he knew he'd done something wrong, but he also knew that he'd soon be getting his forgiveness hug! Bless him, I just couldn't resist the golden boy.

As I went to hang up his collar, I looked at his nametag to discover that it was nothing to do with the way the lady spoke, it really did say 'Spik' Well, I had to laugh, as I was pretty sure I knew exactly what had happened. Iain – that's what had happened!

When Iain came home that evening, as always, he called 'Hi honey, I'm home' I was in the kitchen making him a cup of tea, and he asked how my day had gone.

'Well, it was pretty uneventful until I had a phone call from a very well-spoken lady about Spik!'

'Spik?' he said.

'Yes, Spik's been up to his tricks again, only this time, he went to the big house, and did a bit of frolicking with their girlies!' At first, I thought it was either the way she spoke, or couldn't read the tag properly when she said Spik, but no, she was spot on!'

'What are you on about – Spik?' he asked.

Tongue in cheek, I told him about our little incident, and pointed out to him, that the name-tag, did indeed say Spik.

'Ah yeah, right, err, Spik' he mumbled. 'I forgot to mention that. I didn't have enough room for an e, so I left it at Spik. I didn't think for one minute that anyone else would see it, Sorry, I forgot to tell you' So, after another good laugh, we decided that 'Spik' would be added to his long list of his various 'nom de plumes!'

1991 wasn't all hearts and flowers though, as in June, my beautiful mum passed away… even when you think you're prepared for death, nothing can take away that feeling of pain and emptiness. Mum had never really recovered from the stroke she had in 1985, and being a fiercely independent lady all her life, she hated the fact that she had to rely on others. I owe so much to this amazing lady. She used to make up songs and stories when I was young and did it all over again for her grandchildren! She could make me laugh, even when I was in stroppy teenage mode, and determined not to. She had the gift of knowing what to say and when to say it, and always had a cuddle ready should any of us need it -and even if we didn't we'd get it! I miss her wit, wisdom, hugs and smiles and feel so privileged to be her daughter...

TILL THE NEXT TIME...

Throughout his life, Spike was completely healthy, never needing more than annual vaccinations, flea treatment and worming. Not bad for a pup who almost died of Parvo Virus! He developed Arthritis in his later years, but it didn't stop him from getting around, albeit slower than usual. People don't believe me when I tell this tale, but I promise you – it's true. The vet had put him on Rimadyl, an anti-inflammatory, and Easy –Flex chews. We had never had any problems with giving him anything, he was always obliging where food was concerned.

Then, one day, as I was emptying the water from the mop bucket down the drain outside, when I noticed little pink bits all around the rim. It looked like wet powder that had dried. When Iain came home, I asked him too, but he couldn't throw any light on it either. Then I had a thought...

The next time we gave Wigs his tablets, we watched him, and were amazed by what we saw. The crafty canine walked to the drain, had a quick look around, and then spat the pink coloured, Rimadyl tablet down it! I could not believe what I was seeing!! I always thought he was a clever boy, but this was quite incredible! How did he figure out how to do that? Nobody had shown him. Mr. Wigs was far smarter than any of us thought!

So unfortunately, for all the wrong reasons, Rimadyl tablets really were money down the drain!

Inevitably, the day came when his poor little body had had enough, slowly, slowly it began to function less and less, until…

I remember it as though it was just yesterday.

I looked towards my husband. Like me, he was choking to fight back his tears… There were no words we could say to comfort each other, we were both heartbroken. The young vet who administered the euthanasia, (with such care and compassion) suggested we left via the back door. We were extremely grateful for this, neither of us could have faced going through the waiting room, where Spike had stood only a little while ago. More tears, one last cuddle and the promise of eternal love, we stood up and left our beautiful, golden boy lying silent on the red tiled floor…

The hider of socks, eater of shoes and killer of balloons, the most faithful of hounds, he was a total fruit loop, but we loved him with all our hearts. He blessed our lives for fifteen years, and there is not one minute of that precious time that I regret. He lives on in our hearts, and we have some wonderful, treasured memories and one or two (hundred) photographs!

We'd tried so hard to convince ourselves that it was for the best/kindest/ thing to do etc., but now we felt like murderers. How I wish we had not had to make that decision. Certainly, up to that point in my life, it was by far, the worst one.

Once outside, we stood and sobbed, arms wrapped around each other for some kind of solace. We stood for ages, trying to avoid the inevitable journey back to our empty, Spike-less house. Just for that moment, time seemed to stretch out before us, and the prospect of long, empty days without Spike filled my heart with utter despair. I must try to get a grip, after all, I'm the mommy, and I'm the one who has to be strong for my boys. They were both going to need some serious cuddles when they came home from school, and boy, would they get them!

We decided we simply couldn't go straight home, so despite the weather being miserable, we decided to pay a visit to the Burghley Horse Trails, in nearby Stamford. This annual event draws in thousands of people over the three-day period. There's always so much to see and do there, we thought it might take our minds off things, and cheer us up a bit. Big mistake, for when we arrived, it seemed that everyone had a Golden Labrador with them, everywhere we looked, we saw him, and so the exercise was futile, and a waste of money, so we had a coffee, blew our noses and left for home.

As soon as we opened the door, the house didn't feel right. No welcoming woofs, no waggy tails, just a deafening silence. We just sat looking at each other, neither one of us knowing what to say, and try as I might just couldn't get those images of Spike out of my head. Strange isn't it – why we always seem to relive sad moments in our lives, when we know it's only going to cause more sadness and pain.

It all started again when the boys arrived home, it broke my heart to see them so sad. They knew that there was a chance he wouldn't be home, but I guess like us, they were hoping for the best. Breaking the news to the boys was incredibly painful, I would have given anything not to be the one to tell them, but it had to be done. In a way, they were expecting it, but we all know, that even when you think you are prepared for the worst, to be told it had actually happened knocks you sideways.

My poor boys were absolutely gutted – they had grown up with the wonderful Mr. Wigs, and I knew they would miss him as much as we would. I hate seeing my boys so sad, and like lots of other mothers, I'd willingly take their pain/sadness if I could. It hurt to see them hurting so much, but I reminded myself, that death is really a part of life and eventually, everyone will experience loss - it's all part of growing up... But deep down, I knew that this huge, Wiggy-shaped hole will be with us for a long time....

We then had the distressing task of putting his things away, and the tears started all over again. Only another dog lover understands how deep the pain goes. For weeks after, I seemed to be hoovering up his hair, each time I cried like a baby for my beautiful boy. We had lost one of our own – a very special, precious member of our family.

The day he died, blossoms came out on the apple tree in our garden, the one he used to cock his leg against. It's not meant to bloom in August. It had never bloomed at that time of year before and has never done it since. A sign perhaps? A couple of weeks after, we buried Wiggy's ashes in the garden, just under the tree where he liked to sit. Every week from then on, I would place a little flower or something over his grave and tell him how much we loved and missed him.

I hope our wonderful Wigs knows wherever he is, how very much he was loved. No dog could have been loved more. ....We vowed and declared we would never, EVER, have another dog and suffer this unbearable heartache again. That was'till **he** arrived...

SPIKEY THE PIKEY

It never fails to amaze me, how we parents' always fall for our off-spring's tales of woe? Each time I am caught out on one of their 'yarns' I swear it won't happen again. However, like most self-imposed promises, I fall in hook, line and sinker, especially where my boys are concerned. I'll never learn!

It was now 1998. Terry was still living at home at the time, but Chris had moved away a couple of years earlier. Initially, he had moved to the next town to train as a Chef, but it didn't last very long. I think the long hours interfered too much with his personal life! I mean - fancy your employer expecting you to work in his restaurant over Christmas and New Year, how very inconsiderate of him! I think he had bitten off more than he could chew – if you'll pardon the pun!

Now, a couple of years (and jobs) later, he was sharing a house with some friends in Coventry. It wasn't exactly a 'des-res' nor was it in what you might call a 'sought after area,' but it was a roof over his head. He certainly met with some remarkable characters whilst he was there, but the most remarkable of had four legs!

The four-legged one first came to our attention, when Chris decided to move on to pastures new, and relocate to Milton Keynes. He felt that he would have more opportunities there; goodness knows he'd had no luck in Coventry, so it was time to move on. Everything seemed to be going well – he'd secured a job and somewhere to live, there was however, a small problem - a four-legged problem, e.g. 'No dogs allowed' certainly threw the cat among his pigeons! He didn't want to give up the four-legged one, he loved him to bits, but he really needed to move, so set about hatching a 'cunning plan!'

Miles away from Coventry, I was at home sitting by a nice, warm fire. It was a bitterly cold Thursday afternoon in early November. Autumn seemed to have bypassed our little part of the country this year; it was certainly cold enough to be mid-winter. I was languishing on the sofa, snug and warm watching the lunchtime news, and feeling quite pleased with myself, because all my jobs for the day were done. Just the shopping to do tomorrow, then the weekend can begin. I was just having a swift ten-minute siesta, when the phone made me jump out of my skin!

'Hello' I said rather shakily.

'Hello Mum' replied my son.

I immediately recognised the voice of baby number two – Christopher.

Back then, when the youngest baby rang, he would go through a series of statements. This, in turn, would determine how the conversation would go – what he wanted. These preliminaries consisted of saying hello, telling me how much he loves me (ah bless!) and how I am, without a doubt, the best biddy in the world (yeah right) were usually followed by -:

1. I need...

2. I want...

3. Would you be able to...

4. I could do with...
   and the one he practised most often,

5. I'm skint!

However, this day, he didn't use any of his conventional templates he just went straight for the bullseye!

Both my sons call me Biddy, Bid or The Biddy, and Mum is reserved for those special occasions when a little extra creeping is called for. I was onto him immediately!

In those days, mobile phones and answering machines weren't as prevalent as they are today, if they had been, I could have had my very own answering machine for the boys. It may have gone along the lines;

"Thank you for calling the Best Biddy hotline. Your call is important to us, so in order for us to process your call efficiently, please choose from the following menu: -

If you are calling to inquire about the Bid's general wellbeing and welfare – press 1

If you are calling to ask a favour – press 2 and choose your words carefully.

Press 3 if you are planning to visit (please note – this number's a bit dodgy) Please confirm your reservation 24hrs before travelling.

If you are calling to ask for a loan, press 4 – move the phone away from your ear, and wait for the laughter to stop!"

If you are calling to repay a loan – don't press anything- just dash round to your mothers' immediately and pick her up off the floor!"

Maybe I ought to patent that idea? Ah well, back to Christopher's phone call.

'How's it going most excellent Mum in the world?'

(Here we go!)

'I've got a bit of a problem' he said, 'I need (ah, he wasn't going to disappoint me after all!) could you to do me a gigantic favour'

'Oh really, and how much is this 'gigantic favour' going to cost me' I asked

'Oh no, I don't need money (music to my ears!) I'd like you to take care of something for a couple of weeks.' (Note: a COUPLE of weeks)

'Well, I'm sure I can manage that, although it really depends on what the something is?' I told him.

'Well, I'm moving to a new house; going to live in Milton Keynes, got a job lined up and everything, but I'm not allowed to take my dog, as it's no pets allowed, so I thought I'd ask you to have him – just until I get settled like, and find somewhere where I can take him.'

'Hang on a minute, did you say dog?

YOU have a dog? I didn't know that. What flavour is it?' I asked him.

'Ah Mum, you'll just love him! He's clean/house trained/obedient/well behaved/only small and he doesn't' bite!'

'What do you mean, he doesn't bite? What sort of dog is it?'

'He's a two-year-old Staffy and he's gorgeous! I've called him Spike in honour of our Spike. He's actually called Prince, but I think Spike suits him much better. Spikey the Pikey's been here, there and everywhere - I'd seen him several times before and he is so cute. Poor little guy has had two different homes. When I heard that he was being sold, I just had to have him! I can't wait for you to meet him'

He was talking so fast; my brain was having trouble trying to keep up with what he was telling me.

'When you say 'Staffy', do you mean as in Staffordshire Bull Terrier? I asked.

'Yeah' said Chris 'He's a right little live wire.'

'I'll just bet he is' I replied. 'I don't know Chris, I'm not sure I could cope with another dog, let alone a Staffy, I'm a bit dubious of that breed, and I don't think Iain will be too keen.'

Back then, I, like many other misguided people saw Staffies in the wrong light – A shark on a leash; aggressive and nasty; the Anti-Christ of the Canine world; The devil's disciple! Why would anyone in his or her right minds want to keep a dog like that as a pet? I am pleased to say, that since then, I have eaten my words. Several hundred times!

Ah bid, don't say no just yet please? You haven't even seen him. Ask Terry about him, he loved him, and he'll help you to look after him (Oh really? I think not!)

Please Mum pleeeeeeeease, I'm desperate! I don't want to part with him, he's my little buddy and we've been through a lot together. He's the most important thing in my life – he's all I've got. Don't say no just now, think about it and I'll call you back!'

Before I could answer him, he'd rung off. Crafty little devil, he knows how to get around me. Chris is a black belt in the art of manipulation. He knows the old 'think about it' routine usually gets results. I wanted to help him out, of course, but a Staffy? I just wasn't too sure about that, but the one thing I was sure of, was that Iain would be dead set against the idea.

I thought back to that August day a few years ago and remembered the pain that had come with it. That pain was still as raw today as it had been then. Could I afford to let myself get attached to another dog? Chances are, I'd be seeing quite a lot of him, but still, I suppose a couple of weeks wouldn't hurt, would it? It would be a bit like having Grandchildren: Spoil him rotten; give him back!

Yes, I suppose I could look after him for a couple of weeks, I'd have to meet him first though – I wanted to see what I was getting into before I made any promises, and most importantly, I had a feeling it might be hard to sway Iain. I would get straight onto that when he came home from work. I would have to dust off my womanly wiles!

I suppose I should mention at this point, that Christopher is usually known as Griz, short for Grizwald. Many years ago, just before Iain & I were married, Iain decided to take us all out for dinner to a nearby restaurant. At that time, Chris's table manners (like most other 11-year-old boys) needed a considerable amount of fine-tuning, and was generally, not fit to unleash onto the unprepared, unsuspecting general public! At that time, Terry was only marginally better house trained!

I warned the pair of them before we left, that I expected nothing less than good behavior and polite table manners. Failure to comply with this request would result in possible injury, unimaginable punishment, and I would ground them 'till they were pensioners!

Iain arrived to collect us, and we headed off for the restaurant. It was the first-time Iain, Terry, Chris and I had been out together to a restaurant as a family, and I was really looking forward to having all my boys together for a special dinner. It was December, and because of this, the restaurant had a set menu, which consisted of traditional Christmas fare. It did not however, include chips! I mention this, because that was all that Chris wanted – Chips! He was on one of those horrible finicky childish fads, where he wasn't happy unless his meal included chips! He would have had chips for breakfast with his Ready-Brek had I allowed it!

We all tried to persuade him that he would enjoy a meal without chips, but his face was long, and I could sense a challenge. His bottom lip was out so far, it was almost poking me in the eye. He was working his way up to a full -blown strop, so I gave him one of my 'wait till I get you home smiles' (the grimace through gritted teeth look!) and told him, that if he didn't choose something quickly, then he could go and wait in the car. He didn't like the sound of that, so he reluctantly put his lip away, and ordered his food. We managed to get through the starter without too much fuss, and then the main course arrived.

Everything was laid out in separate dishes and looked very appetising. Suddenly, Chris's face lit up, with the arrival of a bowl of parsnips. They had been cut up a la Julienne, and he thought they were chips! We said nothing, as he dived into the bowl. To be fair to him, it was an easy mistake to make; the lighting was rather dim in there. One mouthful confirmed that they weren't chips, and the lip returned along with the puckered brow.

At this point, I intervened, and reminded him that the offer of being grounded was still available, unless he bucked his ideas up! Very grudgingly, he made an effort, and ate most of what was on his plate, so was rewarded with the dessert menu. Iain asked for the bill, and we stood up to put our coats on. As I moved my chair out, I caught sight of the floor underneath our table where Chris had sat. All I can say is that whoever sat at that table after us, wouldn't need a menu – just a quick glance at the floor would establish what was on offer!

It was like a war zone down there – bits of food, parsnips, and peas, in fact a bit of everything he'd had to eat. I was NOT amused! Terry could see that I was lining up the flight path to go into orbit, so he started laughing and said, 'He's like the entire Grizwald family rolled into one, in fact, from now on, I'm gonna call you Grizwald!' Being Christmas time, we had just seen the film 'National Lampoon's Christmas Vacation' starring the haphazard Grizwald family, and believe me, the name was very appropriate, and suited him down to the ground!

I must say, the name stuck, and he still gets called it to this day – except by me. I call him all sorts of things – depending on what he's been up to – but usually, we call him Chris. If he's in trouble, its Christopher, and if he's in it up to his neck, it's Christopher Thomas!! I have been asked on more than one occasion why I had named him Grizwald! People really think that's his name. One little story springs to mind.......

One day, whilst he was living in Coventry, I needed to speak to him, so rang the number he'd left for me... A young girl answered the phone, so I asked for Chris.

'I'm sorry, you must have the wrong number, there's no-one here called Chris.'

'Are you sure?' I asked, 'this is the number he gave me, shall I read it out?'

I rattled off the phone number, and she said.

'Well, that's definitely this number, but I'm sorry, I'd like to help, but I just don't know anyone called Chris. Maybe it was before I started living here?'

Well, he had said he was moving, perhaps he'd already gone?

Just then, I was aware that someone else was with her.

'Hang on a minute Mrs., one of the lads had just come in, I'll see if he knows him.'

I will never forget what came next. I heard her speak to the lad who'd just come in.

'Hey Griz, do you know anyone called Chris? There's some woman on the phone after some chap called Chris who used to live here - do you know him?'

I almost fell off the chair laughing! She, like a lot of other people only knew him as Griz! What IS he like????? No, better not to answer that!

Anyway, I digress, Back to the cunning plan...

Dinner was almost ready when Iain arrived home that evening. Most evenings, I have a cup of tea ready for him, but this night, it was beer.

'What have you broken?' was his remark when I presented him with a beer.

'I don't know what you're talking about, why would you think I've broken something just because I have a beer ready for you?'

'Because you usually have that's why!'

The cheek of it, as if **I** would do a thing like that!

As I busied myself in the kitchen, I was working my way up to broaching the subject of 'operation canine'. I decided to just get it over with and ask sooner rather than later. I elected to go for the direct approach, but eased myself in with the usual daily pleasantries: - How was your day? What did you have for lunch? Hasn't it been cold today? Is there anything interesting on TV tonight? He nodded and smiled to each question until: -

Oh, by the way, I said we'd look after Chris' dog for a few weeks'.

That got his attention! I knew he was staring at me, but I had to compose myself before I could meet his eyes. Unfortunately, I have the most annoying habit of laughing when faced with a dilemma, and I knew it would blow my chances if he saw any hint of a smile.

'A what?

Did you say dog?

Who's got a dog?'

Whose dog is it?

That's my Iain – why ask one question when several will do!

'Well actually, it's Chris' I said. 'He rang this afternoon, He's got a new job in Milton Keynes - sounds promising, AND somewhere to live, but he can't take the dog. He seems quite taken with him, and really doesn't want to part with him, I think he's got himself well and truly attached to it'.

"Didn't even know he'd got a dog, since when did he get a dog?' Iain muttered 'What made him get a dog? He can barely look after himself, let alone a dog. How's he going to afford to look after it? Food, vet bills, etc., No, I don't think so, I don't really want another dog here, it would be too upsetting' And they say women go on!

Poor Iain, did he really think I would just accept 'no' until I was sure he really meant it?

Like most of the female species, I struggle to accept the negative gracefully. I have to be absolutely sure that I've given it my best shot and pursued all avenues from every angle. Sometimes, re-packaging the question, and approaching from a different slant works, and if all else fails – I have been known, on occasion, to resort to bribery! I did not intend to accept defeat this early in the proceedings!

'Upsetting?' I asked 'Why upsetting? I think it might be fun. Be nice to have a dog around the place again.'

At this, Iain departed upstairs to change. He needed to go and think of some suitable excuses as to why we couldn't have this dog. I think he knew he was going to be overthrown, and just wanted a little more time to re-arm and make me sweat a little.

I got on making dinner for us. Luckily, it was one of Iain's favourite dishes – Chilli Con Carne. Get some of that down his neck with a couple of beers, then bring out the big guns! Like the boys, I too had a special sentence, especially reserved for those 'puppy eyed' moments, when new items of clothing/shoes/handbag were 'needed'.

By this time, I was looking forward to having the dog, and had re-considered my line of attack!

When Iain reappeared, he didn't look quite as intimidating – the work suit now replaced with tracksuit bottoms and a sweatshirt. I knew in my heart that I could persuade him to have this dog, but I didn't really want to do that. I wanted him to want him; it would be much easier in the long run.

He was watching the six-o-clock news when I told him that dinner was ready. He didn't speak as he took his seat at the dining table. Bless him, he is the one who ultimately makes important decisions, (or so I let him think!) but I so wanted to help Chris out with this little dog. I thought back to the earlier phone call, when he'd also gone on to tell me how this dog was the most important thing in his life, and how much he meant to him.

'What sort of dog is it?' Iain asked. (Bingo! Here we go!)

'It's a little Staffy, about 18months /two years, and he's had it about six months' I replied,

'Staffy, as in Staffordshire Bull Terrier' he sounded stunned 'Aren't they one of those dangerous dogs?'

'I don't think so'

Gosh, I really wasn't sure, and hoped that my uncertainty didn't show.

'No, I think you're thinking of the Pit Bulls'. Again, not having had a dog for a few years, I was somewhat vague as to which dogs were on the Dangerous Dogs list.

'Let's assume that it isn't a dangerous dog. After all, it can't be that dangerous if Chris's had him for six months- it would have eaten him by now! It should only be until he can find somewhere to live with him. I know it might take a bit longer, there again, it might not even be for two weeks, and he might get lucky.'

'Yeah, right' he said sarcastically 'We might win the lottery on Saturday too!'

'Oh well', I said 'At least I can tell him I tried' (time to launch my secret weapon; a tried and trusted ancient, traditional method used by women the world over!)

'I thought you might quite enjoy having a plausible excuse for a walk down to the pub' (Light the blue touch paper and stand back! I noticed a flicker in his eyes; - the information was being passed to his brain, to begin processing. This could take a while, as I knew it would involve some pretty intricate calculating, e.g. The number of beers he'd be able to have - divided by the number of nights he'd be able to go out - times the hours he could prop up the bar. Something along those lines I'm sure. I knew that all was not lost. - Not yet!

We ate the rest of our meal in silence. I could almost hear the cogs of his brain ticking over. An unrestricted pass-out to the pub............. no time limits, I just knew he wasn't going to pass up a golden opportunity like that! As I went about clearing the table, he went to watch the rest of the local news. I thought it best to leave him to mull things over about the dog, but now, I was a little more optimistic about the outcome. The jaunt to the pub was a stroke of genius. The bait was far too tempting to refuse. We don't use carrots and sticks in my house – just beer and whisky!

Later that evening as we settled down to watch some television, he started to ask me questions about the dog.

'So, how old did you say it is? Are you sure you would be able to manage with your neck/back?' That's my main concern.' Funny how, it was now me that was the issue, but, I couldn't very well protest when my welfare was seen to be his prime concern.

I'm sure I can manage' I said, 'I'll have a darn good try, and if there are days when I can't take him, maybe you can when you get home'.

'Well, I suppose I could manage a little walk with him. I'm not really thrilled about this, but I suppose we could give it a whirl. But no whinging if it messes in the house.'

Me? Whinge? As if............ Result!

The day after, I rang Chris first thing in the morning to tell him the good news. I was so excited; I couldn't wait to meet the little fella! Spike mk. 2! How wonderful!

We arranged that Terry would drive over to Coventry and collect him the following day, which was a Saturday. This was good, because Iain would be home, and we would be able to spend a little time with Spike before leaving him on his own. I had a part-time job, three afternoons per week, so, he would have a few days to get used to his new surroundings before he was left 'home alone'.

Come Saturday morning, we had our usual cup of tea in bed, and watched the news, but I wasn't in the mood for relaxing, I just wanted to get down to the market. There was 'doggy stuff' that needed to be bought.

Didn't take me long to sniff out the pet stall; Iain, bless him, just looked on with a sympathetic look and a slow shaking head! He knew it was futile telling me not to buy this or that! It appeared that Spike, like his recently acquired owner, travelled light and didn't have too much in the way of luggage. Poor little soul slept on Chris' bed, so we needed to buy him his own. Things had changed somewhat, since I'd bought things for our original Spike., prices being the main one!

I couldn't believe my eyes when I looked around, there were so many things to choose from. I thought I'd better get him a couple of toys too, oh, and a ball (Spiky mk.1 loved a ball) some doggy chow, in fact, lots of doggy chow (I had no idea how much a Staffy ate but went on the presumption that it would be about the same as Spike mk.1). Then there were treats, some of those dental chews – Spike mk1 just loved those. Oh, how about Bonios? Spike used to give us all four paws for one of those! A new nametag, nothing too fancy mind, he is Staffy after all. We'd better put our address on it for now, just in case he runs off. Perhaps a nice new collar – and maybe a matching lead too.

The list went on and, on and Iain, followed close by, carrying the shopping, and said nothing, he didn't need to; the look on his face said it all! In fact, Spike's shopping bill cost more than our food did that week! He knew there was a fair chance that on the way home, a trip to the local pub would be suggested by way of compensation for all this doggy shopping, so he suffered in silence. He learned many moons ago that if he played along with my way of thinking, he would be rewarded in beer! However, there were times when he simply refused to compromise. On these occasions, and I very reluctantly had to accept defeat – till the day after!

I was like a cat on hot bricks waiting for them to arrive. We'd arranged his bed in the kitchen and found a space in one of the cupboards for his chow. I paced up and down between the front and back of the house, willing them to hurry up and appear. Iain, by contrast was reading one of his car magazines. Unbeknown to us then, it would be one of the last times he would be able to read in peace!

HURRICANE SPIKE!

At long last, around four o clock, they landed! As I opened the front door, this whirlwind whooshed through my legs, and into the living room! He ran to Iain, and then back to me, then to Chris, then to Terry, I was exhausted just watching him! He was moving so quickly, I couldn't really see what he looked like. When he came to a standstill, he cocked his leg, peed on the hall carpet, shot off into the living room again, then through to the conservatory.

'Err, hello bid, this is Spike!' said Chris, trying ever so hard not to laugh.

'You don't say' I replied, 'you were right when you said he was a 'live wire'. What does he do for an encore?'

As we chatted about him, he finally came to a halt, and lay down on the carpet in front of the fire. I was able to have a good look at him as he was still. The first thing I noticed was his huge mouth with a very long tongue, dangling from the side. His white face had a few little black spots on the forehead. He looked a bit like a canine version of an old, Winston Churchill, but without the cigar!

As for his tail; - well, it hadn't really stopped wagging since he came in!

He made us all laugh, as his tail not only wagged from side to side, it went up, down and round and round too! A serious contender for a 'Waggiest Tail Competition!' He was brown and white, and considerably smaller than his predecessor. His huge head and legs were white, and the rest of him was brown, except for the very tip of his tail, which was white. He looked as though he was wearing a little brown waist-coat, but overall, he was cute – really cute!

I went into the kitchen for a floor cloth, which I gave to Chris.

'Your dog – your mess, so you get to clean up after him.'

'I thought you might like to get a bit of practice in!' he laughed.

I went back to the kitchen to make some coffee, and the dog was almost there before me. He was like greased lightning and skidded to a halt behind my legs.

'He's probably thirsty' said Chris, so I got the newly purchased bowl, and filled it with water. This seemed to be quite acceptable, as he gulped it down, he managed to cover everything within a 3-foot radius!

'Do you think he's hungry' I enquired.

'He's always hungry' laughed Chris, 'He could eat a sack of potatoes more than a pig, and still go looking for more!'

'Shall I feed him then? I asked, 'What time do you usually give him his dinner?' At this, the Staffy started a wagging frenzy, and went around and round chasing his tail.

'He knows what that word means said Chris, 'the 'D' word, so you'll get no peace until you've fed him. He can keep this up for hours, so it's best to just give in and give him the chow.'

I hurriedly produced a tin of Pedigree Chum, opened it, added a handful of mixer, and set it down in front of him. This also seemed most acceptable, and he got stuck right in. Minutes later, the food had disappeared, and all we could hear was the sound of the metal dish being knocked about the floor, as he tried to find one last morsel. He looked up at me expectantly. I told him, 'If you're looking for a pie, you're out of luck pooch!'

'He's a hungry nosed little devil isn't he' I said to Chris 'When did you last feed him? Anyone would think he hadn't had a decent meal for weeks!'

'Like I said, he's a pig!' he answered 'He'll eat anything you put in front of him. Speaking of which, you might want to reconsider that dog food; - the after effects are gross, - could melt the enamel off your teeth if you get too close'. So **that's** the rather unpleasant odour permeating the air. 'I'll bear that in mind' I said through a screwed-up nose!

All this excitement eventually took its toll on the Staffy, as after a lightening sprint around the garden, peeing on everything in sight, his batteries finally ran out, so he and his little 'stink cloud' settled down in front of the fire for another quick nap. Spike had his own cloud long before Amazon!

Iain had said very little during the performance and was now staring at 'Hurricane Spike' in amazement. I had been so concerned about getting the right food for the dog, I'd forgotten about people food! Iain came to the rescue and offered to go to our local 'chippy' to get fish & chips for us all. This would, of course, be after he'd had a little 'walk' with the dog to the pub; best introduce the little fella to his new environment! (Yeah yeah bla bla bla…) He spoke as if he was doing me a favour, but I had known that that 'pass-out' wouldn't stay blank for long!

'Well, if you're sure you don't mind? I said, playing along with his game 'that would be lovely',

'Of course not, he's probably ready to stretch his legs after being in the car.'

'Well alright then, as long as it's okay?'

The boys decided to accompany him (surprise surprise) Bless them! As they were leaving, I reminded them that they were walking the dog, and that he wouldn't be able to stretch his legs very far in the bar! They had the cheek to laugh at me!

A couple of hours or so later, three bedraggled looking men bearing fish, chips, and one highly excited, panting Staffy arrived home. The dog was here, there and everywhere, sniffing throughout the house. As soon as I started opening the chips, he appeared. The sound of rustling paper like a magnet to him.

We chose to eat our chips on lap trays – big mistake! The trays were almost exactly Staffy head height, and he was more than a little interested in what we were eating.

Chris just glared at him and said-

'I do hope you're not **SCROUNGING**!' the emphasis being on the word scrounging.

At this, the Staffy cowered away, tail between his legs, and sat by the fire, and although he continued to stare at us, he kept a respectable distance. Long distance scrounging! Umm, that's one sentence to be stored away for future reference!

After we'd finished eating, I followed Chris into the kitchen to find out more about Spike.

'So where did you get him from' I asked.

'well, to tell you the truth, I won him in a game of cards!' he replied.

'What??? You played cards for an animal; how could you!'

'Mum, let me explain…

Spike's owner and I were playing cards at a mutual friends' house. The lad had been saying that he needed to sell the dog, as he could no longer afford to keep it. Anyway, when the time came for him to 'pay-up' he couldn't, so told me to take the dog in lieu of payment. No-one else would take him, so I ended up with him, but I'm really glad I did!'

'So, what does his owner say to this?' I asked.

'I don't know, I haven't seen him since that night, and I've no idea where he lives. Anyway, it's his loss, he's a cracking little dude!'

Why am I not surprised? Just when I think it's safe to go back in the water… it seemed history was about to repeat itself, like the time we went to Germany.

All too soon, it was time for Chris to leave. I could tell that it was hard for him to leave his beloved Staffy, but at least it was better this way. Better than having to leave him with strangers or worse still, leave him permanently. He also knew that he could come and see him, or take him at any time, so I guess that helped his goodbye. Only another dog-lover could truly understand how sad it can be leaving your faithful hound behind, even when it is for the best.

During the rest of the evening, we continued to size each other up. Wherever I went, he would appear, almost like he was scared of losing me. Nowhere was off limits to this dog, even a few private moments in the bathroom were interrupted! He had his big white snout into every-thing!!Come bedtime, and we tried to persuade him to go outside for a tinkle or whatever it is that he did before going to bed. Unfortunately, he was having none of it! I went outside – he came outside. I went back in – he came back in, and not a tinkle in sight! He obviously thought we were playing a game, and there could only be one winner- him!

Eventually, after about half an hour of frantic coaxing, he finally cocked his leg – right on my Rhododendrons! Spike and I were going to be having serious words in the morning. There was only one more game left to play that night; see if I could shut the Staffy in the kitchen and get to bed without him. It took a few attempts, but eventually I had him on the right side of the door.

Our bedroom is directly above the kitchen, and I could hear his claws as he paced up and down the tiled floor. I turned to Iain and asked him if he thought the dog had everything he needed?

'Maybe he's looking for his cigars!' he said. He too thought he had a look of the great man about him! Suddenly, silence...... I lay awake listening for him, but not a peep was to be heard. Bless him; he'd gone to sleep, which meant I could too. I would need a good night's sleep every night in future, to cope with the demands of the 'Dog formally known as Prince'.

I usually start the day off with a cup of tea, brought to me in bed, by my wonderful husband! Being a sharp cookie, he hollers 'good morning' from the bedroom door. He reckons it's not safe to get too close during my awakening moments. He says he could do with a cattle prodder sometimes, to nudge me from a safe distance. I have no idea what he means.

I'm not too sure what it was that actually woke me up. Was it the thud of the bedroom door, as it hit the wardrobe, having been 'biffed' open by himself? On the other hand, was it thud of 18kgs of Staffy landing by the side of me? I guess it was the latter. I didn't know whether to laugh or cry! I tried to hide under the quilt, but he was having none of it, and proceeded to dig me out! His long, wet tongue trying to remove a couple of layers of skin from my face. He was nibbling at any bit he could get at and biffing the bit's he couldn't! I was fairly sure that mornings were going to be slightly different from now on! I was exhausted before I'd even got up! This dog is a master of 'tongue foo!'

Tongue Foo black belt!

As I made my way down the stairs, the Staffy was jostling me. Wherever I put my foot, he seemed to be there. Another step down, there he was, turn to the left, there he was again, turn to the right… You guessed it. This dog must have an award; he's especially gifted at getting in the way! When I got to the kitchen, the biffing took a turn for the worse! I assumed that he wanted feeding, and thankfully, I was right. I gave him some dog chow, and within minutes, it was gone. It was almost as if he just leaned over the dish and inhaled! I've never seen a dog eat so fast. Had I not known better, I would have thought that he hadn't had a decent meal in weeks.

After he'd finished his chow, he trotted off through the living room, belching, grunting and farting as he went. I was left in no doubt as to what his next request would be; it felt like the whole house quivered as his big, white head biffed open the back door. I aimed to get it open quickly; I didn't want to have to replace any broken glass!

He strutted around the garden sniffing and biffing everything in his path. Only after careful consideration, did he choose the perfect spot for his morning constitution – right on top of a dwarf conifer! My plants were on death row!

Ablutions over, he continued his trot around the garden, nose first, sniffing at absolutely everything, I'm sure there wasn't a single blade of grass he left un-sniffed! Showing no interest on coming back into the house, I decided to get on with some chores and leave him to his own devices.

No sooner had I picked up the hoover, than he was at the back door, butting it with his big, white snout! Biff, biff, biff, he was using his head as a battering ram! The entrance to our back garden is directly through the French windows in the conservatory, and although they claim to be shatterproof, I didn't know if they were Staffy proof! He saw me watching him, but I was obviously taking too long to let him in. I opened the door just in time to save them from another biffing!

As I opened the door, he strutted past me and disappeared into the kitchen, and I guessed from the clunking sounds I could hear, he was checking out his dinner bowl, just in case it had magically re-filled itself whilst he was out checking the perimeter. Having found it to be empty, he came into the lounge and flopped down in front of the fire. He seemed quiet enough, so I set about hoovering the living room to get rid of the dog hairs.

Iain suffers with Asthma, so I wanted to help lower the chance of it flaring up. I was concerned that having been without pet hair for so long, it might just start a reaction in him. So, I plugged in, and switched on. With the speed and stealth of an Exocet missile, he seized the suction pipe and began tugging at it. He scared me half to death!!

Concerned about the welfare of my Hoover, I switched it off, and tried to distract him with a tuggy, which he immediately tried to kill. For those of you who have never played tuggy with a Staffy, let me familiarise you with the rules;

He wins – game over!

I left him assassinating the tuggy, and thinking he was occupied, I tried to Hoover the rest of the room, but it was not to be. For there, with his paw firmly down on the tuggy for safe- keeping, he was trying to mutilate my Hoover! It was hard not to laugh at this crazy canine, but I knew I had to show some authority - show him who was boss, but somehow, I just knew that he would disagree with my choice. In the end, I had the Hoover in one hand and the tuggy in the other. We girls are so ingenious when it comes to multi-tasking! Eventually, he dragged the tuggy off into the conservatory where he could kill it in peace, and though I may have won this battle, it was highly unlikely I would ever win the war!

It took me three times as long to get my jobs done, thanks to the support of the over active Staffy! He was in to everything! I remembered when I was little, and my Mum used to say how she wished she had another pair of hands! Like never before, I now understood exactly what she meant. Eventually, he tired of the tuggy, there were only a few, mutilated strand left now, so he went to his bed. We'd now put his bed in the living room to keep an eye on him, so I took advantage of the lull, and made a pot of tea.

As I sat enjoying five minutes peace he had his eye on me, watching my every move, just in case I had something for him.

After a swift nap, a regenerated Spike was ready for the next round of tuggy. I had never seen such strength in a dog!

When Iain and Terry came home, they took over the Staffy entertainment programme. Terry produced a rubber tuggy for him to play with, and Spike wasted no time trying to kill it. He stood there, with a look in his eyes that said, 'come and have a go then' he was very agile for such a solid dog.

Terry played with him for a while, at one point, he even lifted the tuggy up in the air, but the Staffy just dangled from it, nothing between the floor and his four paws, again, the tuggy stayed firmly between his teeth. I was concerned that it would hurt him....... They just laughed at me!

His jaws are comparable to a vice. Once something enters them, chances are it's staying there, until he decides to release it. I soon discovered that bribery was the only way forward with this canine. It's the only currency he understands. As long as the bribe was edible, and waved around in front of his nose, we had an understanding.

If you are very lucky, you may catch him off guard for a split second, only then might you be able to grab the tuggy/toy from his jaws, but my money's on the one with the white head. Every time!

A very good friend, who happens to be another Daphne, suggested I get a rolled-up newspaper to divert his attention, and threaten him if need be. Good idea, I will leave one on standby in the conservatory. She had been round to meet him, and he charmed her within minutes.

It wasn't long before I had to use the rolled-up magazine – he was trying it on with my Hoover again, so I whipped out the old TV guide. It only took seconds for him to swipe it out of my hands and rip it to bits! That's what he thought of Daphne's idea. He laughed in the face of rolled-up newspapers!

The second weekend, we decided to take him up to the fields and let him have a run; after all, with the two of us to keep an eye on him, there shouldn't be any problems – right?

Wrong!

There are several places around where we live, where it's both safe and secure to let a dog have a good run. We're very lucky in that respect, but I was worried about letting him off, because I knew that I wouldn't stand a cat in hells chance of catching him if he decided to jump ship, and at times, there are sheep and horses kept in some of the fields. Not that I would let him loose near them, but he wouldn't know that he wasn't allowed in there if he ran off, and I didn't want to think about the consequences.

Chris said he had no road sense, but believe me, it wasn't just 'road sense' that he lacked, he didn't seem to have any sense at all!

Armed with pockets' full of chewies, we stood a fair distance apart, undid his lead, and put him in the middle. Initially, things didn't go too bad – I called him, and he came, then Iain called him, and he ran to him. Each time, we gave him a little chew and told him he was a good boy. After a while, he must have gotten bored with the game, as the next time I called him, he ran towards me, and straight past! He ignored Iain too. He sprinted off at a great rate of knots, as we stared after him in disbelief.

We shouted to no avail, so set off running after him. He vanished into a tall yew hedge, and we were relieved a little, for we knew there was a stile on the other side of it that would/should stop him in his tracks. We walked the rest of the way, believing the gated stile would stop him took the pressure away, but when we went through the trees, there was no sign of him.

We made our way to the end field, where all the water from the surrounding fields accumulates after heavy rainfall. We had had lots of rain lately, so chances are, that field was going to be pretty full; Very deep by dog standards.

Salty old sea dog

Where on earth could he be? Then, we heard barking in the distance – we knew it was him. The little devil wasn't going to let a gate stand between him and some water, he'd obviously biffed it open with that huge head of his! Thankfully, the gate was still in one piece!

I believe that most dogs can swim, but I didn't know if he could. Sometimes there were sheep in this field. Were there any there today? What was he barking at? Visions of an outraged, seven-foot farmer with a two -foot rifle sprang to mind!

I needn't have worried, there he was, cool as you like swimming around in the 'lake'. He barked when he saw us, almost like a child shouting 'look at me mum.'

Up and down, round and round he went, barking all the time, his tail acting like a rudder. He was having an amazing time. We tried to coax him out, but he was having none of it, and carried on swimming. Just as I was thinking that I'd have to wade in and grab him, he swam towards me. Hallelujah!

Tired and bedraggled, we dragged him out. He was absolutely freezing, but it didn't seem to bother him. We dragged him home, and dried him off, then he settled down for a while – just a little while, then he appeared with his tuggy and started biffing my legs. Oh joy!

He wasn't too tired to biff the cupboard door for his dinner later either. It hadn't taken him long to figure out where the chow was kept, and after he'd finished dining, he moseyed past us en-route to the garden. A good sniff later, he came back indoors, sprawled out in front of the fire, and there he stayed, stinking the night away! I thought he would be quieter after all the exercise he'd had, but alas, I was wrong; yet again, as after forty winks, he was up for a game of tuggy! I have to use both arms to do this, as he's so powerful, he would have me on my rear end in no time! No peace for the wicked!

A few miles up the road from where we live, is an old, disused airfield. It was a very busy, important landmark during the Second World War, but today, it lies quiet, abandoned and still. The runways are in disrepair, but it is surrounded with trees, and makes for a lovely, safe walk, especially with a four-legged friend. Deer live there too, and it's always a thrill to see one. Another plus for this location, is that no matter how many cars are there, you might not see another person on your walk. Because of the wide-open spaces, you always have plenty of warning to the approach of other people, thus allowing plenty of time to put Spike on his lead before meeting up.

One of the many things we'd learned about Spike, was that he just loved to go in the car, so, seeing as how the weather was fine and sunny despite the time of year, we decided to take him up there and tire him out. As soon as the door was open, he leapt in, and after his customary pacing of the back seat, he found just the right spot and settled down for the ride.

When we arrived, he was eager to get out of the car, and as soon as the door was opened, he leapt out. The airfield is only accessible by foot, so we kept his lead on until we got to a safe place, and then let him go. We began to throw his ball, but he showed no interest whatsoever, he was far too busy sniffing around. Then, he found a big stick, which was far more interesting! The problem was getting it off him. Only a big stick will suffice - half a tree preferably! He'd bitten it so hard, that his eyes were bulging out, and his tongue was bleeding, consequently, as he shook his head, he covered himself in blood, which looked real impressive on his white face.

He looked like something possessed; I prayed that we wouldn't meet anyone! I had visions of kids kicking and screaming while fleeing from the demonic looking dog, who surely must be one of the devils' disciples!

Spike's little stick!

In the blink of an eye, he lost interest in his stick, and bounded off down the runway. We called him, but he ignored us. We shouted and shouted, but still, on he went. By this time, we too were running, in fear of losing him, although the airfield is safe, it is also quite large, with many places to lose a dog.

Out of the blue, he veered off to the left, and disappeared. Oh, my God, I thought, if he doesn't slow down, we'll never catch him. I expected to hear screams from the direction he'd headed any minute! Still, at least it would give us a clue as to where he was heading!

After what seemed like miles, out of breath, energy and patience, we found him – well we heard him first. A strange barking sound, not like his usual one, this was kind of hoarse. As we got closer, we could hear splashing, and there he was – swimming around in what could only be described as a filthy, stinking, toxic mud pit. Just the way he likes it! He was having a whale of a time, and I'm sure if he could, he would have waved us in to join him! Bless him!

We collapsed on a relatively clean bit of grass and watched the performance. Although by now, I knew he was indeed a very adept little swimmer, I wasn't too sure how deep his latest find was. However, both Iain and I were shattered after our sprint (Iain only ever moves that fast when they call 'last orders at the bar'!) so we began calling him to come out.

'Spike... Come on Spikey boy' –

Nothing, he didn't even look at us.

'Spike' I called in my best 'mum's not very pleased voice' 'Don't make me come in there!'

– still nothing.

I tried a different approach in a more subtle, melodic voice that always used to work with the boys.

'Oh Spiiiikkkkkkeee- Spiiiiikkkkkkeee, come here boy, come on, there's a good boy, don't make me come in and get yooouuu!

At last, an acknowledgement from the hound, but after a few quick barks and a good wag of his tail, he went back to attend to his business.

Finally, I fell back on the tried and trusted way – bribery!

Out came the chewies, and out came the dog......................
Eventually! I think it was only when I pretended that I was going to eat the darn thing that he decided to get out! He loved these little marrow-bone chews and went through a funny ritual whenever we gave him one. He didn't like to take it from your hand, you had to throw it to him. After which, he'd pick it up, throw it in the air a few times, knock it about with his head, and only eat it when he was sure it was dead. His little marrow-bone chews became known as 'rat biscuits'!

What a sight he was! The thick layer of squelchy, slimy mud completed the look. His white bits were black, his brown bits even blacker, all in all, with the bulging eyes; he'd give the creature from the black lagoon a run for his money! We hadn't considered this when we decided to visit the airfield. Consequently, we were unprepared. No towel, in fact nothing to dry him with. I could have choked him!

We set off back to the car, but a slightly different longer way, in the hope that we might find another, cleaner 'pond' to relieve him of all the stink that he'd acquired, and boy, did he stink!

The gods were smiling upon us, as just a couple of miles down the path, we found some clean water. Without any hesitation, in he went, but this time, we encouraged him to splash around, and the two of us kicked water all over him. Oooooh this was a good game, and fortunately, this water was no more than a huge puddle to us, so we had no problems getting him out. Wet through and still stinky, but at least he was clean and stinky, so we went back to the car.

My car at that time was my pride and joy - A metallic blue Renault 19. Not just any old 19 though, this one had once been the demonstration car for Renault U.K., and we were lucky enough to be the first owners of it after they had finished with it. It had all the latest gadgets and gizmos on it, heated leather seats, electric windows, but sadly, nothing to get rid of dog stink!

NOT WIRED UP RIGHT

Christopher's couple of weeks turned to three, then four, and before I knew it, it was almost Christmas. During this time, Spike and I developed our own little routine. He learned that when he came in after his first visit to the garden, there was food waiting for him, so he didn't hang about! He almost hovered around the garden on three legs, squirting anything that didn't move. My plants were looking sad, as no matter what we did, he still preferred to pee on them. I guessed their days were numbered – his pee must be like battery acid! After his breakfast, he'd trot into the conservatory in search of a little ray of sunshine to warm his tummy.

On my three workdays, Spike would take me for a walk after his nap in the mornings. The days I didn't work, we had two walks – weather permitting. Some of the locals we encountered on our daily outings gave us a wide berth and a lot of sideways glances. I told them all that I was just 'doggie sitting' and there was no need to- worry, he wasn't vicious. I must admit, he looks kind of fierce, but looks can be very deceiving in animals AND humans. If only they knew he was just a wuss bucket!

Later that month when Chris came to visit, I told him what had happened with the mud-pit, which he found highly amusing.

'Oh yeah, I forgot to mention, He **LOVES** water.'

(Now he tells me!)

'But we weren't actually near it, he just ran off and found it, and it was quite a distance away too, I was shattered' I told him.

'You'll just have to remember to try and keep him away from water next time you're out. At least you'll know where he is' he laughed, 'he's like a homing pigeon!'

'So, as long as I know where every pond, puddle, lake, stream, river and swamp is, I'll be fine!' I quipped. 'No worries then eh.'

That's all I need, a daft dog crossed with a homing pigeon!

'Is there anything else that we should know while we're at it?' I asked Chris.

'Err, no, I don't think so. I take it you didn't B.A.T.H him when you came back from that walk?'

'What are you on about? .... B.A.T.H… You mean did we give him a bath?'

How I wish I had had a video recorder ready to film what happened next.

As Chris & I stood talking, hurricane Spike came whizzing past us, almost knocking my legs from under me, and leaving a trail of destruction behind him.! A bowl of Pou Pourri went for a burton, as did the mat it was stood on; then came the 'Biff'. Such was the force of said 'biff', the bathroom door handle left a mark on the cupboard! This dog's a menace! After a few grunts, there followed, what can only be described as a pathetic whinge. 'That dog of yours is not right' I said, 'he's completely round the bend.'

'he's not wired up right!' laughed Chris 'It's because you said 'bath, he knows what it means, and to him, it means water and he'll sit there whinging until someone turns the tap or shower on.'

I put my head around the bathroom door, and what a sight to behold; there, with his big wet snout as close as was physically possible to get to the tap, sat Spike.

It was like he was possessed. He didn't even blink when we got close to him; such was his concentration on the tap. He was making some peculiar noises, a cross between a grunt and a high-pitched squeak – almost like a pig! A scrunt!

'He'll stay there until someone turns the tap on' chuckled Chris.

'Well, let's get it over with then' I replied as I reached out and released the water. As soon as the water began to flow, the dog went wild.

I'm not sure whether he was trying to eat it, bite it or kill it, but he was intent on doing something to it! His huge snapping jaws trying to devour every single drop.

I was fascinated watching him and amazed by his determination.

'He won't try and eat me if I turn it off, will he?' I asked, having suddenly thought on, that every drop that disappeared down his throat would reappear later on, and judging by the amount he'd shifted, it was promising to be a busy night for the door attendant! 'Nah, you're quite safe, but throw a towel over him, otherwise you'll be wet through' said Chris.

Tap off, Chris and Iain proceeded to get him out of the bath. Not easy, especially since he wanted to stay in. Eventually, we had him in front of the fire drying him off, after which, he sprawled out on the rug, and fell sound asleep.

I could see there was potential for lots of laughs between Spike and the bath. Not that I'm a teaser.

My Mum used to tell me that when I was young, I was a real tormenting little devil, but in a nice way. Coming from a large family, I came in for a considerable amount of teasing when I was a child. My brother is nine years older than I am, so you can imagine the goading that went on. However, having grown up with one of the masters of mockery, my mum, it was inevitable that some of this would 'rub off' on me. My mum wasn't averse to a bit of kidding!

Babies, young children and pets don't stand a chance if the mood takes me. Baby toes simply have to be nibbled and tickled, and I consider it a divine obligation to blow raspberries on their tummies! I love to see the look of a little ones' face, after hearing one of my totally outrageous fabricated tales that range from Billy Bow to Ginny

Green-teeth! I'm quite good a spinning a yarn, my poor boys were shown no mercy as they were growing up!

I remember an incident, which Terry has probably still not forgiven me for, and will cringe unreservedly when he reads this! He was desperate to start school, but after he'd been there a couple of months, the novelty had worn off, and he wanted to stay at home with his brother and me. I didn't want to upset him, but he had to go to school, so I told him, that if he was a good boy and went to school, I'd let him have a day off. And, if he was very good, I'd make it two! He fairly skipped down the road to school for the next few days, thus earning his two days off, but boy, was I in big trouble when he realised that no-one went to school on Saturday and Sunday!

So, back to the Staffy stinking on the rug - well, I just needed to see if it was a fluke with the bathroom, or whether he had an afterburner hidden under his tail. He was sound asleep, but the temptation was too great, so I shouted across to Iain, that I was going for a bath.

He was like Usain Bolt hearing the starting pistol! He was up and away in the blink of an eye, like a short-range ballistic missile; his mission – the bathroom! Bless him; he went through his routine again, biff, thud, squeak, and grunt. This time though, there was no official turn on of the tap for him, but I felt he'd earned a reward, so brought him a rat biscuit, which he was more than happy to get out for.

'You're a bad biddy' sniggered Chris, as I giggled away,

'I can see that you're going to be a bad influence on my dog if I leave him here too long. Speaking of which, I might not be able to take him until after Christmas if that's okay?'

That statement brought me straight back down to earth with a bump; until now, I hadn't thought about Spike going, it saddened me to realise that inevitably, in the not too distant future, he'd be leaving us. He'd been with us for about six weeks now, and Iain and I had completely fallen in love with the Staffordshire fruit loop!

Later that night, after Chris had left, I asked Iain what his thoughts were, as we both knew it was only a matter of time before Chris wanted him back, and neither of us wanted to think about that.

'I won't half miss him' Iain told me, 'I'd forgotten how much fun dogs are to have around, he's such a comic!'

'How would you feel about getting one of our own?' I asked 'you know, once he's gone. I know we said we'd never get another dog after our Spike, but if we got a Staffy, we wouldn't be tempted to compare them too much.'

'No, you'd just compare it to this Spike, and I'm pretty certain you won't find another one like this, he's a one off' Iain replied.

Now, just because Iain said 'no' doesn't mean that that would be the end of it, Oh no, not by any means! I have many tried and trusted alternative methods on hand that I can resort to if necessary. Some of them involve beer, and depending on the scale of the need, a wee dram of his favourite whisky! Christmas was around the corner, and we all know that a dog is not just for Christmas!

I always look forward to the festive period; both the boys and their partners come and stay with us. Chris was bringing his new girlfriend Sarah along to meet us, which I was looking forward to. There's always plenty of food, drink and laughter, and we all enjoy ourselves. This year was going to be extra special, having Spike with us. Spike mk1 loved to be given something wrapped up and would spend ages ripping it open. I was quite excited wondering how the Staffy would react. I could only imagine!

Very soon, Christmas Eve was upon us. It dawned brisk and frosty, but not a sniff of any snow. Iain was already on holiday and Terry came home at lunchtime. Chris arrived mid-afternoon with Sarah completing our little family. We both liked her immediately. She was a lovely girl, with a brilliant sense of humour – which she would certainly need being with Chris! Each time someone arrived, Spike would greet them like a long-lost friend, running around in circles and chasing his tail. When I went into the kitchen to start preparing food, he was my best friend. Around 5.30, Iain and the boys decided that it might help get them into the festive spirit, if they took the dog for a quick walk to the pub, besides which, Spike would like a walk. Really?

Over the years, I've learned that 'quick' and 'pub' do not sit together easily in Iain's vocabulary, so I knew we were looking at 2/3 hours. Minimum!

Would they like to eat before they went? I enquired. No, they replied, we're only going for a couple, (NOTE: couple!) we won't be long!

Spike however wasn't going anywhere until he'd had his chow, which was finished by the time they'd all got their coats on! Sarah and I decided we'd stay home to watch for the squadron of flying pigs that would be bringing them home!

We were quite happy to have a good natter and get to know each other while enjoying a couple of drinks. Sarah was very easy to talk to, and before long, we were like old friends. Several hours later we heard the key go in the front door, followed by a lot of commotion. Our hallway is quite small, and there were three fairly inebriated adults (and I use the term loosely, very loosely!) and one very excitable dog. They were all trying to get past the dog and open the door to the living room: - quietly!

Anyone who's ever tried to sneak in inconspicuously after a few sherbets, will know, that more often than not, it doesn't work, and the quieter you try to be, the more noise you seem to make!

Now I don't know about you, but whenever Iain comes home late, it's always someone else's fault, how could it possibly be his? It's a trait the boys had readily picked up. I've heard it all (or most of it) during my years with him, and I know he does it to make me laugh. He knows I'm not really cross with him, but I'm hardly likely to confirm that, am I? So, his excuses come thick, fast and sometimes, quite ingenious! But not tonight – I think he was working on the basis that Sarah and I would be in the same state as them. Wrong!

Iain was the first to speak. 'Honey we're home!' he shouted from the hallway.

Spike started barking at the raised voice, then the door opened, and in they fell – all four of them! It was now gone ten and they were gone too!

'Sorry we're late, but... well, we bumped into, err, what's his name Chris?' said Terry.

'Who?' asked Chris.

'The guy who came and stood with us; you know who I mean, the one in the red suit; kept forcing us to drink beer because it's Christmas.'

At this, I smiled a little.

'Don't tell me, he had a huge white beard and some shifty looking dogs with him' I said.

'So, you know him too biddy!' laughed Chris, 'said people call him Santa!'

Amid the commotion, Spike was running about, barking, jumping all over the furniture and generally causing havoc and mayhem! All this, while Iain, Terry and Chris were all trying to justify why they were late back!

I watched in bewilderment at the scene unfolding before me. I turned to Chris and said, 'I think your dog's either blowing a fuse, malfunctioning, or both!' My home had become a mad house!

We noticed that Spike had gone very quiet and disappeared. Strange, I thought, he's usually right in the middle of whatever's going on. Then I spotted him in the conservatory. The little devil was just about to cock his leg on the Christmas tree!

'Noooo Spikey, no no nooooooooooo' I shouted. I had visions of him being electrocuted in a very compromising position! He looked at me, and stopped what he was about to do, and dashed across to me expectantly.

'I don't think he's ever seen a Christmas tree before, certainly not one in a house' said Chris ', Maybe he thinks it's one of his Christmas presents' said Terry 'an indoor loo; how thoughtful of you Bid! 'I got up and let Spike out. It was no good trying to reason with these boys of mine, especially when they've been too long near the barmaids' apron, and I've always believed that if you can't beat them – join them!

Several drinks later, we were all beginning to feel the effects of the 'Christmas Spirit' so I decided to head off to bed and leave the rest of them to it.

For some reason, Spike decided that he was coming with me, and having neither the time nor patience to argue, I let him follow. As soon as my head hit the pillow there was a 'thud' as Spike landed on the bed. He circled around a few times, found the optimum spot, then lay down and went to sleep. I woke as I heard Iain come up and listened to the exchange of grunts and moans that ensued as he tried to persuade Spike to get off the bed! I tried not to laugh as I listened to Iain trying to whisper quietly, 'c'mon Spikeeee, c'mon little lad, let daddy get into bed. Let me in Spikeeee' Ah... so it's Daddy now is it? I'll get plenty of miles out of that!

The following morning, I awoke to what I thought was Iain trying to push me out of bed. As I turned over, I realised that it was Spike who was responsible, as I came nose to snout with him! He had all four legs in my back having a good stretch. Iain, on the other hand, was hanging out of his side of the bed, and judging by the amount of room I had to manoeuvre, it was a safe bet as to who had the most room last night, and I reckon it was the one with the white head!

We did our usual 'Strictly' routine down the stairs, but he beat me in the end. He ambushed me at the kitchen door ready for his breakfast. He was leaning down on his two front paws, with his bum stuck straight up in the air; his tail was spinning round like a rotor blade. He looked ever so funny!

Bacon butties are always on the menu on Christmas Day, and this year was no exception, I'd even got a couple of sausages for Spike as a treat, which he disposed of in seconds, I don't think he even chewed them the little porker! By the time everyone was up, fed and watered, it was late morning, and the moment I'd been waiting for – present time, or rather Spikes' present time.!

He was so interested in the presents under the tree; in fact, we'd had to stop in from trashing a couple on more than one occasion! I did the honours and began distributing the pressies. As I threw one over to Terry, it was intercepted by Spike's head! The little devil grabbed it and ran off into the conservatory with it. When we caught up with him, he had it pinned to the floor with his paw, while his teeth were shredding the paper from it. By chance, I had a couple of chewies in my pocket, so I waved one of them under his nose.

He was sizing up his options. Chewy or present? Present or chewy? You could almost hear the cogs grinding! He was trying to be sneaky, by keeping one paw on the present, and reaching for the chewy! Clever maybe, quick – undoubtedly, but with the dexterity of a house brick, he scored high in clumsiness category, and although he was reluctant to part with his swiped present, the sight and smell of the chewy won in the end, it usually does. Chewies and water over-ride everything!

When we gave him one of his presents, he went crazy! First, he killed it by throwing it up in the air; he then annihilated all the wrapping paper, before finally finishing it off by de-squeaking it! Squeaks never last long with our dogs!

Christmas lunch was a pantomime – at every twist and turn in the kitchen, there he was, behind me. (Oh, yes, he was!) However, I didn't spill or drop anything on his head, though I'm, sure he would have liked me to! We decided to give him his very own Christmas Dinner, and I had filled his bowl with turkey, a few veggies and some gravy. The plan was to give it to him after we had eaten, it didn't quite work out that way!

Happy Spikmas!

He soon got down to business, working the table like an old pro. First to one, then to another biffing our kneecaps with his wet snout. I knew exactly what he wanted, and if I was to get any peace, I would have to admit defeat and feed him! I know dog trainers everywhere will be in full cringe mode because I gave in to him, but what the hell, it was Christmas!

I was a little concerned that his dinner might not be quite cool enough for him. I needn't have worried; he got stuck into it before my hand had quite let go of the dish, so I left him to it. The sound of his empty bowl being pushed around the floor alerted us to the fact that his nibs had finished dining, and no doubt would soon be back for an encore. He didn't disappoint me, just when we thought it safe to relax, 'biff' – there he was again with that huge snout!

I thought he would have wanted to curl up and sleep like the rest of us, but no, he had his own arrangements for the afternoon, and they didn't include sleep! Unfortunately, you just can't ignore a Staffy, try as you might, he just won't be ignored, so while the rest of the family settled down to watch the Christmas film (whilst checking the inside of their eyelids), Iain and I were playing tuggy with one of his new toys. Spike joined in too!

It was advertised as being totally durable, but there's durable, and there's Staffy-proof, and they aren't quite the same! Luckily, tiredness finally took its toll on the boy, and he snuggled down for a quick nap, and thankfully, so did we.

All too soon, the silly season was over, and it was time for Chris to leave. Although Terry lived with us, he too had to go back to work, so we tried to get ourselves back into a routine, which was somewhat 'Staffy' orientated! The weather was pretty appalling, but it never deterred himself from his daily walkies. I'm sure he didn't even notice it was cold, as he demonstrated one day up in the field.

A tractor had been through and left huge ruts in the ground. Earlier, they had been frozen, but had now started to slowly thaw. Spike thought these were wonderful, as he bounded through them leaving a wake of water and ice. His paws cracked right through the ice, but he didn't care less, he was having fun, and I had to resort to bribery to get him to come home. He's a sucker for chewies!

He was absolutely wet through by the time we arrived home, and sadly, one of his paws had been bleeding a little, but he didn't seem bothered about it. After a good rub down, and a little bit of fuss, he settled down in front of the fire with a chewie stick.

One day during January, the dreaded phone call came.

'Yo Bid' said my youngest.

'How's it going?'

My mummy senses were tingling, and I waited with baited breath to hear what he was going to say, but if I am truthful, I already knew what was coming.

'I'll come and get Spike at the weekend if that's okay? I've moved again and the lad I'm sharing with is more than happy for me to have Spike'.

I managed to say, 'Ah that's nice' before that awful tightening sensation at the back of my throat started, you know the one - the tightening that precedes tears.

Although I knew what the answers would be, I still had to make sure.

'Are you sure? He's into a nice little routine now, he's used to going out at certain times, and eating at 6, he's not used to being on his own now'.

Any excuse I could think of came out, but Chris was having none of it, and the more I tried to talk him out of it, the crosser he became.

'Look Mum, I appreciate what you've done, but he is my dog, and I do want him back. You knew when you agreed that it was only going to be a temporary arrangement. I'll be there on Saturday. See you then' the phone went quiet, and that was it. I knew he was upset as there was no goodbyes, love you or anything.

We would only have this wonderful, amazing, mind-boggling crazy canine for two more days. I cried buckets! I dreaded telling Iain, as I knew that like me, he'd become very attached to the little guy. I was mad! I had promised myself that I would NOT get too attached to this pooch and look at the state of me – eyeballs leaking for England, and a snotty nose to boot! I would defy anyone not to love this dog, he really is unique. I also didn't want to run the risk of Iain saying, 'I knew this would happen'.

Iain arrived home from work to his usual fanfare of a Staffy barking! Not content with barking like normal dogs, he had to jump up onto the settee, and then put his front paws onto the coffee table so that he could see out of the window. It always amused us to watch this performance, and even today, sad as I was feeling; I couldn't help but smile at his routine. I tried looking on the bright side, but apart from the fact that my coffee table wouldn't have to endure four paws bouncing on it, I couldn't find one.

Iain knew as soon as he looked at me that something was wrong. Unfortunately, I'm one of those people that look absolutely hideous when I cry. My eyes swell, my nose goes red, and overall, it's not a good look. We're talking proper mirror breaking stuff! It takes days for my eyes to un-puff, so I really do try very hard not to cry. But when Iain came in and put his arms around me, I just dissolved!

He held me while I poured out all the hurt about Spike, who by the way, was alternating between chasing his tail, and biffing his dinner bowl, totally oblivious to the situation. When he realised that his cavorting was being ignored, he took direct action and biffed the back of my legs! I guess he was telling me, that no matter how sad I was feeling, he still wanted his dinner!

The dreaded Saturday came around, and Chris phoned to say he was on his way. I was determined not to get upset, after all, he was Chris's dog, but boy, I was SO going to miss him.

I could feel the dry throat starting as I collected his bits and pieces, bed, food, collar, lead, toys, (CD collection, cigars, stink cloud etc.) There was only one thing I had to say to Chris when he got here, and that was, if he ever decided that he couldn't look after Spike any more, for whatever reason, he was to phone us immediately, and NOT let someone else have him.

When I heard the car pull up outside, and my heart sank. I knew I was being silly, after all, he was Chris' dog for goodness sake, but I just couldn't help myself. I tried really hard to be pleasant, but it was hard work. I knew how Chris had felt at having to leave his beloved pet, I'd been in that predicament myself, and I also knew for sure now, how my parents felt when I went home to reclaim Mr. Wigs.

Terry had arrived to say goodbye to the little fellow; he too would miss this little firecracker! Spike had gone mad when Chris came in, and soon, we were all laughing at him. Chris was a bit sheepish, and didn't seem to want to hang around for too long. I guess it was for the best...

We tried to make polite conversation, mainly about the dog, and after a quick cuppa, he loaded up his car, and said goodbye. Spike was very happy to go; he loved a ride in a car, so he trotted off quite happily down the garden path. Bless him, the little soul hadn't a clue that he wouldn't be coming back.

Sadly, we watched them walk down the path towards the car. The sight of Spike jumping straight into the passenger seat made me smile, and I tried to console myself by thinking he'd be back to visit sometime, I really hoped he would...

We waved till the car disappeared off into the distance, and then retreated into the house. All three of us glassy eyed. That little dog had touched all our hearts and made us realise our home was just a house without a dog. We would seriously have to consider getting one of our own; we all agreed it was time – time to move on...

But little did we know, that wouldn't be the last we saw of Spikey the Pikey – oh no, not by a long chalk!

JAKEY BOY

Try as we might to get life back to some sort of normality, it wasn't happening, no matter which way we looked at it, we both missed that little whirlwind immensely. His biffing, nibbling, barking, and most of all, the fun he brought to our lives. I wouldn't go as far as to say we missed 'everything': there was one thing in particular that I didn't miss- the repercussions of dog food! Every time I saw another dog, it would remind me that I didn't have one, and echoes of losing our original Spike once again. Coming home to silence was unbearable – a dog-less house wasn't a happy home.

We still had his bed, which Chris had decided to leave behind. I couldn't bear to move it into the shed and justified this by saying that he would need it when he came to visit, and I didn't want it getting damp! There was no two ways about it; it was time to revive the 'bow-wow song' The fact it was a Friday gave me a good start – send him to the pub first!

I found no resistance to my suggestion whatsoever; Spike had really got to Iain, so much so, that we began looking for a dog the very next day. I proposed that we try for a rescue dog, thus helping it – and us.

It's quite rural where we live, and miles away from any animal centres, so we scoured the local newspapers. Eventually, we found ourselves at a place in Leicester, and they were pretty busy! I can only commend these people, particularly the volunteers for the sterling work they do with the animals. These individuals deal with everything from cruelty to abandonment on a daily basis. It takes a very special person to do that – I don't know if I could, I'd be wanting to take them all home with me!

As far as animal cruelty goes, well don't get me started!! Personally, I would string up the wicked, senseless, heartless evil bastards, and forbid them from ever keeping so much as a worm. Period!

I cannot, and never will understand how people can ill-treat or abandon a trusting, defenceless creatures. Sadly, some animals have become kind of a fashion/personal statement, and unfortunately, there will always be the slime balls, which, having no respect for the animal's life, feel they can be discarded as you would an old item of clothing that no longer fitted. I appreciate, sometimes there are exceptional circumstances that are both unforeseen and unavoidable, but there is NEVER EVER any excuse for cruelty. If you take on an animal, you have to adapt your life, and make provisions for any events or unforeseen circumstances that may occur. People not prepared to do this, shouldn't have one.

I'll put my soap-box away .... For now!

So, there we were, trawling around the kennels, looking for a Staffy! Sadly, I would have had every last one of those little critters, had I been able too. It's so heart-breaking to see them in those cages, but there again, I guess these are the lucky ones.

Eventually, we came across a Staffy, and what a little cracker she was! Her name was Bella, and she was a brindle. As we stood watching her, she went to the back of her cage, and dragged her bed to the front, tail wagging continually. It was almost as if she was saying 'come on, take me home with you, I'm all packed and ready!'

I took it as an omen, and after a few minutes, we decided that Bella was worth further investigation.

We went to the office to inquire about her, but our hopes were dashed when the lady told us that Bella was already spoken for. I was gutted! She went on to explain, that sometimes, it didn't work out when potential owners took the dogs home, so, she took our name and address, and promised us, that should things not work out for Bella, she would ring us.

The phone call never came...

When I got home, I rang my very dear friend, Daphne, and told her where we'd been. I had known her for many years, and one of the many things I loved about her, was her attitude. She called a spade a spade, but in the nicest, possible way. One of her sayings was 'there are no problems – only solutions' That's all well and good, but what if there WAS no solution? Her reply to that statement is unprintable! 'never mind kid (she always called me kid) Bella obviously wasn't meant for you, but if you don't get another dog soon, I'm gonna buy you one myself, cause I'm sick of looking at that miserable face!'

She had fallen under Spike's spell just like the rest of us, and she knew how upset we were to lose him. He used to go crazy when she came to our house, he loved her to bits, and never failed to make her laugh. Not bad for a self-professed 'cat' person!

Not long after our visit to the dogs' home, we were out and about doing our shopping. Iain was with me, which is unusual, as like most men, he hates shopping! However, there is usually a method in his madness, that I knew only too well. He felt that he deserved a treat for trawling round the supermarket (and his point is? I do it several times a week!) In addition, where Iain's concerned, there's only one thing that will suffice. Beer! To be honest, I don't like to drink at lunchtime (and he knows this!) so I offered to drive. (Aren't I good?)

We made our way to one of his favourite watering holes where they serve a decent pint, and very tasty food. Linda was on duty behind the bar that day, and as always was welcoming and friendly. As she poured Iain's pint, I told her about our fruitless search for a Staffy.

"You are so not going to believe this, but d'you see that couple at the end of the bar? Well, they have just told me, not five minutes ago, that they are getting a Staffy pup! Not only that, but the people who own the puppies, will be coming in later!"

This was truly music to my ears; Iain's too, as it meant he'd get to stay for a few more pints! I was so excited, hopeful and anxious –

maybe they may have sold them all already? I needn't have worried, although I must confess, that by the time the couple arrived, I had a stiff neck, due to swiveling my head around every time the door opened! It was an omen.

Linda pointed out the couple to us, and there was no stopping me – I was off down the bar to where they sat.

Paul & Anne were a lovely young couple, and not only did they have two puppies available; they were Red, which was the colour that we really wanted. The pups were only a couple of weeks old (ahhhh) but were happy for us to visit and check out the pups! We made arrangements to visit them during the week. I couldn't wait; God was certainly smiling on me today!

I counted down the hours until Thursday came, and we could go and see the puppies. I was like a child on Christmas Eve! As soon as Iain got home from work, I chased him to get changed and eat, and then at last, we were on our way. Melton Mowbray isn't too far from where we live, and although we only went there occasionally to shop, it didn't take us long to find their home. As soon as we went in, we could hear the unmistakable sound of squeaking puppies! I was desperate to get my hands on one! Anne showed us through to the kitchen, where they had cornered off an area for Meg and her 5 pups, which had been born on April 15$^{th.}$

Meg was trying to get a bit of peace when we went in, but the pups were having none of it, as they constantly vied for pole position in the feeding queue! Poor girl, she soon put them in their place.

We watched these tiny little souls in total amazement; I could have stood there for hours, I was completely captivated by them – way off the top end of the cuteness scale! Now some people hearing this next bit say "no way" but I promise – it's true. Having already chosen a name for out pup, I knelt down closer to them, and said.

"Which one of you puppies is called Jake?'

They all turned at the sound of my voice, but one pup pushed its way towards me, and as I leant over to stroke it, Anne picked him up and looked at him, then told me, that this little guy was the only male that they had left. Another omen!

Ok, so I know this kind of thing only usually happens in fairy stories, but trust me, it really did happen, and from that moment on, Iain knew his fate was sealed; there was to be no going back – that puppy was mine!

I took him from her and breathed in that unmistakable puppy smell as I cuddled him. He was so tiny he fitted in the palm of my hand; only about the size of a Guinea Pig, but oh boy, he was simply adorable. He had the familiar, Staffy white flash on his chest, spreading up to his chin, a teeny smudge of white on his nose, and his tiny, little toes, but overall, he was red. He fell fast asleep in my arms; I had fallen in love! Iain though he might have to surgically remove the pup when it was time to leave!

I whispered in his ear "Hello Jake, I hope you don't mind, but I'd like to be your new mummy. You and I are going to have SO much fun, we'll go for long walks in the woods, take you to the seaside, take very good care of you, and we'll love you to bits!"

Iain just lowered his eyes and shook his head as usual when confronted with embarrassment.

As expected, the time just flew by, and soon it was time to put my baby back with his little canine family. but before I placed him back with the rest of the litter, I kissed his little snout, and promised him we would be back for him when he was old enough to leave him mummy.

Anne suggested that we might like to visit again the following week? - I could have kissed her. She didn't need to wait for a verbal answer; my expression told her all she needed to know!

She also said that it would be a good idea to bring a blanket or something along too, so that it could be put in with the puppies to get their smell, therefore, comforting to him when we take him home. They certainly knew their stuff! I would never have thought to do that, but it made perfect sense.

I was in a world of my own on the way home, mentally making lists of things that he would need, and things that he might like. Iain just nodded and smiled, here we go again...

Anything for a quiet life. I couldn't wait to get down to the pet shop, so as soon as Iain' had gone to work the following day, I was off like a shot.

A new pet shop had opened, so I was interested to see what they had to offer. I found all sorts of things for every kind of domestic pet. The one area I wasn't tempted to buy anything from, was the clothing section! Now, I have been blessed with a sense of humour, but alas, I think I would need considerably more than I've got to buy 'dog-togs!' Dressing dogs up in miniature replicas of adult clothes just strikes me as a little odd. I've no objection to dog coats, but frilly pink stuff & combat gear, what's all that about??

I could have done with a large brandy (purely medicinal of course!) when I saw some of the prices, which ranged from the sublime to ridiculous, to out and out more money than sense! Yet, according to the sales lady, they sell quite a variety of dog clothes.

'You'll find the prices are very competitive' she informed me.

'I'll take your word for that' I replied, 'but I think I'll stick to treats for now thanks.'

I bought him some puppy chews, food and a couple of squeaky toys (which I just knew I'd regret later!) A collar, lead, and two stainless steel bowls, completed my list and then I headed back to the car.

I was just picturing the look on Iain's face when I told him about the dog togs. Maybe I ought to wind him up and tell him that I was buying Jake some little booties to keep his paws warm? Or perhaps some ear-muffs for when the bad weather arrives? Best not to think about things like that whilst driving, I'll be in a ditch through giggling before I knew it!

I had become like a child waiting for Christmas Day to arrive! There was a huge red circle around the 1st of June; which was the day we would finally get our puppy, and I was already counting down sleeps! Iain had arranged to have the afternoon of the first off, so that we could spend some time with the pup. I must confess, I found it very difficult to sleep the night before we collected him, I was so excited, worse than both my boys put together!

Fur baby Jake

As the day finally dawned, I was wide awake very early, and eager to go and get our boy. The weather was beautiful, and everything was ready for Jake to come home! I ran around the house, making sure everything was done, as I didn't want to have to do any housework for a few days, I wanted to bond with my pup! I willed the hands of the clock to move faster, but time just seemed to drag.

At last, Iain rang to say he was on his way home – yippee!! I was ready and waiting when he arrived home, but he wanted a cup of tea before we left!! I very begrudgingly made his tea as he disappeared upstairs to get changed.

Finally, we were on our way to get our little lad. I had no doubts whatsoever about taking on a puppy, but on the drive to Melton, I found myself worrying about whether he'd settle with us? Would he pine for his mum and his siblings? I would just have to do everything I could to make his transition as happy as I could.

Anne and Paul were ready for us when we landed. They said they would be on the end of the phone should we have any problems, and they had compiled a little file with loads of useful information for us, which also included all the details about Jakes birth, including what time he arrived, (02.00) and in which order (second of six) He had been registered with the Kennel Club, and I had to smile, when I saw his KC name was, 'Kensid Man of Mischief!' The name said if all!

They really had thought of everything, and I will be forever grateful to this wonderful, amazing couple, who made our dream come true. At their suggestion, we had taken a small blanket to their house a couple of weeks ago, to get the puppies, and his momma's scent on. This familiar smell would help him to settle in.

Finally, it was time to go home, so I picked up our tiny little scrap of a puppy and settled myself in the car. Anne and Paul waved us off, and then I had him all to myself! I was on cloud nine with my baby boy, and it was a wonderful place to be! I wanted to snuggle him, as you would a baby, but Iain growled at me, and said I'd embarrass the dog, so I just held him (tightly) on my lap until we got home. Then I would hug him, and squeeze him, to within an inch of his life!

WELCOME HOME!

When we arrived home, I carried him all around the house, and then gently put him down, so he could explore his new home. I gave him some water, and generally made a fuss – just like a new mum! We took him into the garden, which he really seemed to enjoy. He'd been allowed to play in Paul & Anne's garden with the rest of his siblings, so we just let him be. He was here, there and everywhere. Part of me was concerned that he was looking for his brothers and sisters; I hoped he wasn't going to miss them too much, and prayed that we would make up for it, by being good, loving owners. It was so wonderful to watch this little soul frolicking around the garden, I loved him to bits already. Our future was looking bright, and it was coloured Staffordshire Red!

As bedtime approached, I was wondering how he'd react to being left on his own – would he howl/cry? I was prepared if he did, I had a little blanket in our bedroom for him, just in case. Half of me was hoping he would – just so I could have him in our room! Bless his little heart, he didn't make a single peep, much as I willed him to, he was as quiet as a little mouse. We'd put his blanket and a couple of teddies in his bed, and it seemed he was happy to snuggle up to them.

He was still in his bed when we went down in the morning, and he hadn't left us any pressies! He was a bit desperate to get outside, where he had a huge wee, after which, he came bounding over to us. I was in heaven!!!! I gave him some breakfast, which he demolished in seconds, and then he wanted to play.

We had all sorts of toys for him, but he chose Winnie the Pooh to play with, and set about trying to rip its head off!! He fell asleep mid bite! Just like a baby, my little 'Fur Baby' would sleep quite a lot those first few weeks.

Two little poohs!

We quickly developed a routine, and soon, it was hard to imagine how I'd ever lived without him, it was as though he'd been with us forever.

I was longing for the day that I could take him out, but for now, his collar, lead and harness remained hung on his special little hook, until he was 12 weeks old and fully vaccinated. We'd also signed him up for training classes, which most of his siblings were attending too, now that would be fun!! All those Staffies in one room – bliss!!

The first few weeks flew by and I must say, it was brilliant bonding with our little guy. He was a bundle of joy, a pleasure to be with, and I simply adored him! Anne and Paul suggested that a couple of weeks before we were due to go out, put his lead on, and walk him around the garden, just to get him used to it. He was like a duck to water, no problem at all. So, at the beginning of July, we took him off to our local vets for his very first vaccination. It was a bit like when you take your baby for its inoculation – I was so worried it was going to hurt him, but he didn't even flinch, it was in and out before he knew what was going on. And he got a treat afterwards! We also had an ID chip done at the same time – a brilliant idea, and an unfortunate necessity due to the times we live in.

So now, we were good to go. Tomorrow, we could introduce him to the big wide world – well, maybe just the village to start with!

We took him for a little walk, up to the sports field. We didn't want to go too far with him on his first outing, he only had little legs, and by the time we arrived back home, he fell fast asleep. Bless his heart he was shattered! Tired he may have been, but as soon as he heard Iain opening the gate coming home from work, he was up and at 'em!

A few weeks later, it was time to take him to Obedience classes. All but two of his litter went as well, so you can imagine the mayhem when they all met up! I'll swear they remembered each other. All they wanted to do was play and took very little notice of us at the start – they were the juvenile delinquents! Trust a Staffy to bring chaos where there was calm! The classes were held in Melton Mowbray, which meant going in the car, and he didn't seem very keen on being in the car. This was in the days before harnesses for the car were around, so he went in the back, however, it didn't take him long to squirm his way onto my lap in the front!

It was good to see all his brothers and sisters again, and we sat together in a corner of the room. I christened us 'The Staffia' There were quite a few dogs of all different breeds on this course, but they all learned to get along fine.

Jake seemed to be a slow learner, but he soon caught on once he realised that there was a chewy in it for him – he loved his chewies! I think the course lasted about 6 weeks, but we all agreed, it was money, and time well spent. In a way, it was sad when it ended, knowing that these little souls would probably never meet again....

I would recommend classes to anyone; not only did help us to teach the dogs to behave, it also helped to socialise them. Being Staffies, it was important that they get on with other dogs, and help quash the bad press, that they undeservedly get.

Sadly, no matter how cute he looked, and trust me, he really did, there were still biased, brainwashed morons, who would cross the road rather than walk past us. I used to get really upset, and after a while, I stopped saying 'it's okay, he's well behaved and he won't eat your dog!'

Unfortunately, it is usually the owners that need training – not the dog, and as long as there are stupid idiots using Staffies and other breeds as weapons, this stigma will continue.

As the days passed, we played with him, and taught him a few, basic rules. Sit/stay/paw etc., He also learned that when he heard the back gate being opened, it meant Dad was home – and there'd be more fuss on offer. When hearing the car, I would tell Jake 'Dad's home' and he would start dancing about, and jumping up at the window, till he came in. Iain had to stop and bestow tummy rubs, before coming in proper. He had a little performance when Terry came home too. He loved playing with Terry and would get so excited when I told him he was on his way home to play with him. Terry christened Jake his little 'Bitey Buddy' as he loved to bite his boots. At the time, he worked as a HVG driver for a huge haulage company, and was provided with a uniform, part of which contained safety boots. Being a little over six feet tall, he needed large boots, and Jake was just fascinated with them.

Whenever he got chance to bite them, he would! When Terry came home from work, he would knock on the front door, and shout Jake. As Jake pelted towards the door, Terry would wiggle his hand through the letter box, making the puppy even more desperate to get to him. Jake would go crazy at the waving hand, and there would be rough and tumble once he came in… However, there was something about Terry's boots that he didn't like. The funny thing is, the boots were almost bigger than he was, but it made no difference to his plan to kill them! He probably could have fitted inside one (he almost did one time!) He gave us plenty of laughs with Terry's boots!

Pup in boots!

Christopher brought Spike up to meet Jake, and other than a small altercation, they got on fine. We were a little nervous to start with, as we loved Spike dearly, but he had to learn that this was now Jake's gaff!

I think Spike thought of our home as his des-res in the country. He couldn't understand who the new kid on the block was - what was he doing in HIS house, and most importantly, had he eaten any of his chewies? Spike tried to stamp the paw of authority down, but Jake was having none of it. Thankfully, they sorted out who was the boss (Spike) and then they got on with the important things, like speeding up and down the garden, and mutilating Winnie the Pooh! That was the only spat they ever had.

The day before we got Jake, my brother and sister-in-law (Peter & Nicky) also had a new baby. Theirs came in the form of Bobby, who was a beautiful Collie. Like us, they had lost a beloved dog, Sally, also a Collie around the same time as we had lost our Wigs.

Kissing cousins

Bobby had been born five days before Jake, so they would be pups together. We were eager to get the two of them introduced, so there would be no problems when we went to visit them. Because we lived two hours away by car, we usually stayed for the weekend. We couldn't have wished for better! They got on so well together from the very start, we christened them kissing cousins! We introduced him to the rest of the family, and they all loved him too!

One extended family member was Charlotte, one of our God-daughters, who was eight at the time. She was really scared of dogs, but we didn't know why. When I told Mary S. (her mum) that we were getting Jake, we agreed it might allay Charlottes fears, if she was able to meet a puppy. Although a little apprehensive at first, she fell for him hook, line and sinker, and they became good pals. Thankfully, this relationship lasted and helped to quell her fear of dogs too!

As the kissing cousins grew, Bobby became bigger than Jake, and wanted to dominate, but on the very odd occasion that there was a kerfuffle between them, it was over within seconds. We loved Bobby as though he was our own, and Peter & Nicky loved Jake. Perfect!

We spent many happy hours together with those doggies, even the odd weekend away at the coast. It didn't matter how long they'd been apart, they were best buddies again the moment they clapped eyes on each other. It was lovely to see them playing together. Kissing cousins forever!

BLOOD BROTHERS

Late august, and the weather was wonderful; quite hot, sticky and not much in the way of rainfall. Jake seemed to be growing before our eyes! He was such a good, happy little soul, an absolute pleasure to be with, a joy to take for a walk, and very obedient.

Back then, Iain worked for a large insurance company as a financial consultant, with a young lady called Sara. One weekend, we had invited Sara and her partner over for a barbeque – to make the most of the fine weather. While I was in the kitchen, Iain was in the front garden with Jake. He had found a baby wren that had fallen from its nest in the clematis, which climbed up the front wall. He was going to put it back with its momma. It was a fair way up, so he went off to get the ladders.

I was busy in the kitchen preparing the food and singing along to the radio, when I suddenly realised it was very quiet outside. I called out for Jake, but he didn't come – most unusual. I dried my hands and went to see what they were up to. I shall never forget the sight that greeted me. Iain had fallen from the ladder and was lying unconscious on the floor. A trail of blood slowly trickled down the path, and for a horrible, split second, I thought the worst. Jake was by his side, franticly licking the blood from Iain's head – his little face also covered with blood. I shooed him away, but he seemed very reluctant to leave Iain's side. In my heart, I like to think that knowing his master was hurting, he was trying to make him better; either that, or he liked the taste of blood!

Iain came too as I bent down, and after a few words of reassurance I rang for an ambulance.

I called next door to Heather, my lovely next-door neighbour who took over, calmed me down and stayed with us, until the ambulance arrived. Jake was thrilled to bits with the arrival of the ambulance men; obviously, they had come to visit him – why else would they be here?

Heather looked after Jake whilst we went to the hospital, and thankfully, after a thorough examination and several X-rays, Iain was able to come home. Apart from a broken collarbone, dislocated shoulder and a nasty gash on his head, he was okay – he'd live!

I knew for sure he was feeling better, as, after spending hours in the hospital, the first thing he asked for when we got home was beer – busted!! Can't be that poorly! As I lay in bed that night, my mind ran through the events of the day. Jake and Iain became blood brothers (quite literally) but I know it could have been much worse – we could have lost the wren too!

August was coming to an end, and it was time for the annual horse trials at Burghley House again. It's a wonderful day out, and even if you're not a horse enthusiast, there are plenty of stalls to look around, some of which sell rather yummy food, and a whole cornucopia of various, specialty wares appertaining to Burghley. It was bitter sweet to be there again, as it was August 31st, fifteen years to the day we lost our beloved Mr. Wigs...

One of the many sponsors of the horse trials is a well-known pet food manufacturer, and they always have a huge stand full of current and up and coming merchandise, lots of toys and loads of treats!

Peter, Nicky and Bobby dog were coming with us this year, and once we arrived, it was only a matter of time before we ended up at the pet food stand. Across the front, lay several bowls containing samples of the various foods they produce. Jake could not believe his eyes! He started at one end and munched his way right through to the opposite end, giving sampling a completely new meaning! He took a mouthful and moved along – even bypassing a couple that obviously were not to his liking, before moving on to the next.

He even went back for a second helping of the ones he liked! I know we probably should have stopped him, but it was so funny to watch – he knew what he was doing when it came to his chow! Gentleman Bobby just grazed at a couple. He was never as interested in his food as Jake was. Later, Nicky discovered that he had an intolerance to certain foods and had to be kept on a special diet. Poor Bobs....

Bobby & Jake

Once he'd finished sampling outside, he went on to the stand to see what was on offer inside. He had the cheek to take chews from the staff in there too – gutsy puss! Oh, he loved his chews, however, there were times when his eating habits totally disgusted me!

Living in a rural area, there are quite a few fields where both farm and wild animals live. He loved to sniff out where they'd been, but he also liked to eat what they'd left! He treated the top field like his personal delicatessen, with delightful dishes like Lamb-Pookie, Fox-Faece and Bunny-Bites!!

When he wasn't eating it, he was rolling in it – he really was a little stinker! I certainly didn't want puppy kisses after he'd had a take-away! Try as we might, we could not stop the mucky little devil from eating it! We were told it was something he would probably grow out of, and the only way to stop him, was to keep him on his lead. We just couldn't do that, he loved his run off the lead, so we had to put up with it.

There was one wild animal he really didn't like; Hedgehogs. We think it was because he'd found one in the garden sometime and tried to pick it up. Ouch!

One night on his last patrol of the garden, we heard him making the most awful noise, a really strange bark that we'd never heard before. Initially, we thought he'd hurt himself, and flew out to see what all the fuss was about. He had a poor little hedgehog in his mouth, and he just wouldn't part with it. We tried everything to free the little soul, but he refused to give it up. Eventually, Iain put on some gardening gloves and managed to free the hedgehog, who surprisingly wandered off. Deaf, but still in one piece!

Jake was left with a poorly mouth, as some of the quills stuck in him, and he flinched a little when we had to pull them out. I'd like to say it taught him a lesson – but it didn't! He seemed to know whenever a Hedgehog came into the garden and would sprint off down the path at a great rate of knots! We would know it was when his crazy 'hedgehog' bark started!

Perhaps he had learned a lesson, as instead of picking up the poor creature, he would biff it with his snout. He'd get pretty upset when the little soul left but continue with his weird bark. He would sometimes have little scratches on his nose, but that was about it. However, there must be several deaf Hedgehogs in our village!

In years to come, even our neighbours would know when we'd had a hedgehog in our garden. It was quite funny when they said, 'Jake had a Hedgehog last night then?'

At the end of September, we went to Malta, and left Jake in the capable hands of my younger sister, Beverley. She lives with her husband Michael, and three children Stephen, Benjamin and Hannah. At the time, they didn't have any pets, so we knew he would love all the fuss he would get. I was however, a little concerned when Beverley told me about Gnasher – a dog who lived down the road from them. Just the name summoned up visions of a mean dog, however, my concerns melted away, when she told me he was a Yorkshire Terrier! Naughty little sister!

She and Michael had had a dog just after they got married, he looked like a cross between a whippet and a greyhound. His name was Muffin, he was absolutely gorgeous, but completely round the bend!! (seems most animals in our family are!) One day, Beverley came home from work, to find that Muffin had managed to get into the cupboard under the stairs. Getting in the cupboard wasn't a problem, until she saw what he'd done whilst he was in there! He had eaten a pack of 24 Weetabix – the top tier of their wedding cake (which was wrapped in tinfoil in an airtight tin!) and a large tub of Vaseline!!

Oh boy, did we laugh!! The food was understandable, but Vaseline? We decided he'd used it in lieu of jam for the Weetabix! Beverley certainly wasn't laughing after it passed through his system, and because he'd been thoughtful enough to have the Vaseline, it wasn't too long before it re-appeared! Silly Muffin – what a dog!

Jake didn't bat an eyelid when we left him and was running the household within hours. He soon had everyone reading from his schedule, and kept them amused chasing the pigeons, and being cute. The encounters with Gnasher were all very friendly, providing Gnasher had the last bark! Jake, however, treated this barking with disdain! He'd discovered a new delicacy while on his northern travels, the humble Cow-Pat; he was far more interested in Cow-pats than barking at Gnasher, and took great pleasure rolling in them.

My poor sister was horrified, but Jake's visit had a positive effect, as it wasn't long after his visit, they decided to get their own dog. They couldn't decide between a Staffy or a West Highland White? Eventually, they chose the Westies, and are now the proud owners of two beautiful doggies - Fergie and Tiggy.

LOVE AT FIRST BITE

Towards the end of Autumn, we decided to have a long weekend away in North Yorkshire, a place we both love, before the weather became too bad. Jake had never been overly keen on being in the car, so I sat in the back with him for a while. After a pit stop for necessities, we walked him around the car park perimeter to stretch his legs. When we got back in the car, I got in the front, hoping that he would lie down and go to sleep in the back. After a few miles, Iain noticed something in his rear mirror that made him laugh. Jake had clambered up onto the parcel shelf and was watching the world go by.

For those of us old enough to remember, lots of people used to put toy, nodding dogs in the back window of their cars. Well, we had a real live one!! I would love to have seen the reaction of other drivers when they realised he was real!! Looking back, we shouldn't have allowed him to do it – I certainly wouldn't do it now. But he was quite happy there watching the world go by…

We found a lovely dog-friendly pub in a little village near Pickering. The weather was beautiful; in fact, we hadn't had much rain at all – unlike some summers! The owners had a beautiful Weimaraner called Ellie, who turned out to be Jake's first love! Ellie's mum had hurt her ankle, and wasn't able to walk Ellie, so we took her out with us. Jake was very happy to have a new play mate, it was lovely to watch them bound around the fields.

On one of the days, we had a trip on the North York Moors Railway up to Goathland where they filmed Heartbeat. The steam railway runs along about 18 miles through the national park, and the scenery is stunning. Jake seemed a little bit perturbed when he saw the engine, it must have looked massive to the little guy. Once we were aboard he was fine, and providing we let him sit on Iain's knee and seemed quite happy looking out of the window! Once there, we headed off on a slow jaunt towards the pub. The sun was over the yard arm, and Iain was on holiday – which can only mean 'Beer-O-Clock! The Goathland hotel/Aidensfield Arms is right at the far end of the village.

Fortunately, dogs are permitted so we stopped for lunch, which, if I remember correctly, was very tasty, traditional pub grub. Jake sat under the table the whole time, doing his best pathetic/they never feed me look, and lapping up all the attention he was getting!

Afterwards, we wandered around the pretty, little village, and because we were both 'Heartbeat' fans at the time, we found it very interesting. Soon it was time for us to head for the train back to Pickering. Everyone we met was fussing Jake, and he wasn't complaining! We boarded the train back to Pickering, and again the journey was amazing; there's something about steam engines that is quite magical, and I can understand why there are so many enthusiasts.

That evening, we left Jake snuggled up in his bed, whilst we went down for dinner. When we went up later to check on him, he hadn't moved. Our little guy had had a busy day!

After breakfast the following day, we took Jake and Ellie for their walk. Ellie could run like the wind, and Jake, - well, he could run. He could run right underneath Ellie, such was the difference in size, but no way could he catch her. Still, it was fun watching him try!

It was during this walk that he hurt his eye. We could see that it was uncomfortable for him, but just thought that he'd got a bit of dust in it from the fields. However, when we got back to the pub and bathed it, we saw that it was considerably more than a bit of dust... A piece of straw had lodged itself into his eye and was causing him some real discomfort. The Landlady rang her vets and got us an appointment immediately. The Vets wasn't too far away, and we were there in around 20 minutes.

The Vet was waiting for us and set about examining Jake's eye. He was incredibly good about this, but sadly, he wasn't going to be too good when it was pulled out! Because this would be a very delicate procedure, the vet decided it would be much better if Jake was .

So, our little man had the first, of which would be many, anesthetics. We were behaving like over anxious parents, as it seemed to take such a long time. We needn't have worried, the vet brought out our rather sleepy little Staffy, and I cuddled him all the way back to the pub.

By the time we arrived at the pub, he seemed to have forgotten all about it, especially when he saw Ellie, but sadly, there would be no walk that evening for them. Jake was still under the influence of the anaesthetic and a bit wobbly. However, he was happy to let Ellie see his 'war wound' when she came to give him the once over.

The following morning, they had a little run together in the garden at the back of the pub, and then it was time to leave. It's a good job dogs don't have the same sentiment as humans, as I think both Jake and Ellie would have been very sad to know that they wouldn't see each other again...

On arriving home, we informed our vet as to what had happened, and took him for a check-up the week after. It was looking good – nothing to worry about, it was healing beautifully; The Yorkshire Vet had done an excellent job!

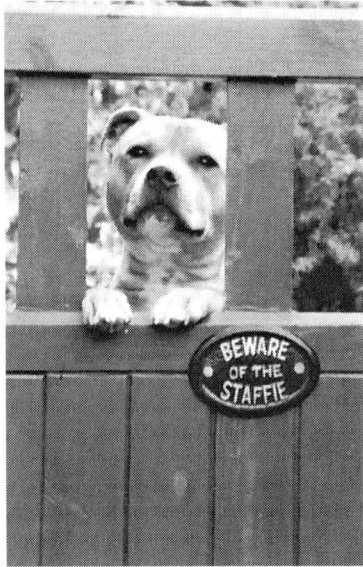

Beware indeed!

We briefly thought about breeding with Jake, as he had a pedigree a mile long, but then we thought about all the dogs in rescue centres just waiting for a forever home and decided against it. I had no doubt that any puppies he sired would have been absolutely gorgeous, but it was not for us (I would have kept the lot!) So .... being responsible owners, we decided to have him 'seen too'.

At the time, our eldest son Terry was dating a lovely young lady, who also happened to be a vet nurse. We discussed getting Jake castrated with her, and she reinforced our thoughts that this was the best way forward. It also eliminated any chance of testicular cancer and would stop his 'doggie urges' so we made the necessary arrangements.

By now, Christmas was just around the corner, so we opted to get it done before. On December 13th (wasn't a Friday!) we took our little guy for his op. Knowing that he knew someone who would be looking after him post op, made it easier for us. We dropped him off at 8.30. I had to give him a kiss before I left him – Iain just laughed at me. When I got home, the house felt so very empty. I looked at his little bed, and his half-decapitated Winnie the Pooh, and once again, wondered how I had ever lived without him.

Every time the phone rang, I thought it might be the vets with bad news. I just couldn't help myself! When they did ring, it was to say that everything had gone well, and my little guy was sleeping. YEAH!!!!!! We could collect him at six.

Ten to six, we were both there waiting for our little man, and after several minutes, one of the nurses brought him out. He was ever so pleased to see us, and although his tail was wagging, it wasn't at optimum wagging speed!

He was wearing, one of those awful cones, and he wasn't terribly impressed with it, but needs must, he had to leave it on. Back home, we followed him around for a while to stop him hurting himself. We tried really hard not to laugh at him, but he was so funny trying to walk around. As all Staffy owners know, they prefer to go through things other than around them!

We put his bed in the living room, and there he lay looking quite pathetic. Most dogs are good at doing pathetic, but I think Jake had a degree in it. The look on his little face was priceless. Think big brown, sad eyes and 'peel me a grape cause I'm poorly' I wonder if they have some sort of training course before they leave the litter?

We took him back for his check-up, and have the stitches removed on Christmas Eve. Everything looked good, everything was where it should be, so we were all set for our first Christmas with Jake! Christopher would be coming with Spike too, so overall, we had some serious celebrating to do – everything was coming up doggies!!! Iain's parents were joining us, so we were all ready for a (Grizwald) family Christmas!

Over the years, being a mum with two boys and various other pets, I had seen some prize-winning messes. I didn't think there would be much left to shock me, but nothing prepared me for the mess those two dogs left! A catastrophe of epic proportion! Each wanted the other one's present, and then when they got it, they didn't want it. They wanted everyone's wrapping paper, which they ripped to shreds and spread throughout the house.

They didn't so much want what was **in** the wrapping, they wanted the wrapping! Anything that contained a squeaky just had to be dismembered; when it had squeaked its last, they were no longer interested. My house looked like it had exploded! Was anybody missing? Would I ever see my carpet again?? Where were Iain's parents???

Jake saw his first snowfall too, although it wasn't the snow that bothered him. There hadn't been much of a downfall, but enough so the kids could get their sleighs out. Jake was upstairs, watching in comfort through our bedroom window. He had taken to sitting on my dressing table, so he could see out of the window, and up the street. It had become his favourite spot! Suddenly, he let out such a piercing bark, we both sprinted upstairs up to see what all the noise was about. There was nothing to see. He stood rigid, staring through the window, but at what? He had taken a dislike to something for sure, but we were at a loss. I stroked him and reassured him there was nothing there, then suddenly, he started again. This time, we could see what he was barking at – the kids on their sleighs.

This really puzzled us, he loved kids, so why all the fuss? We discovered the cause later that afternoon, when all but one of the children had gone indoors. A little boy came speeding down the road on a blue plastic sledge. He went mad!

It took a bit of trial and error, but eventually, we learned it was the blue sledge – not the child. Over the rest of winter, we noticed that he was fine with any other colour – except blue! So, the blue sledge (any blue sledge) became 'Blue Dog' You only had to say it, and he was up the stairs in a flash, looking for him out of the window.

We had a lot of laughs when 'Blue Dog' was about!

Another funny little anecdote happened on that Boxing Day too. Iain was taking Jake out for his walk and decided to call in the local pub for a quick one on his way back. Way back then, fox hunting was legal, and still prevalent in our neck of the woods. One of the local hunts gathered on Boxing Day outside our village pub, before setting out on their quest, but I doubt anyone expected to see the 'pantomime' that unfolded that day.

As they rounded the corner to the pub, Jake saw all the hounds and started barking at them. Iain was ready for a quick retreat, but he didn't have to, because all the hounds backed off, and away! It appears everyone was in stitches at the sight of the tiny, little Staffy pup, causing havoc and mayhem, and seeing off a pack of hound's single pawed! Puppy power!

Jake became a legend that day, albeit a very tiny one!

The Landlord at the pub, was a lovely chap called Dave. He'd taken a shine to our little lad too, and consequently, he always had a couple of chews stashed away for him. The funny thing was, where he kept them; - they were in a tankard, hung up above the bar with various other ones, all belonging to different people. So, our little lad had his own tankard, along with the rest of the other locals!

MILLENIUM

Like a lot of other people, I always seem to shed a little tear on New Year's Eve. I think of those I have loved and lost; parents, dear friends, dogs and relatives, and wonder if they are somewhere up in the ether, looking down and saying – "look at the state of her again!"

However, tears or no tears, this was a definitely going to be a very happy New Year, especially with our little guy.

Usually on New Year's Eve, we would wander down to our village pub to celebrate, but this year, we wanted to be home with our little lad, so we did not stay too long, and went back to celebrate with him. However, he had his own agenda; all he wanted to do was sleep, but the nice thing was, he wanted to do it in between us on the settee.

The New Year arrived, and as January progressed, Jake and I carried on with our routine, and began to find different places to go for walkies. Sadly, both Iain and I were working all day when we had Mr. Wigs, we didn't have the same amount of time to spend with him, but Iain came home each lunch time to let him out. He didn't go short of anything, especially love! Life was good, and we were both enjoying having a doggie again – he really was a joy! A couple of months into the New Year, Chris rang and gave us some unexpected but happy news. Things were going really well with him and Sarah, and he was thinking about moving in with her and her family. The thing was, he wouldn't be able to, as her Mum had a cat.

Unless...

Here it comes again…

You're one step ahead aren't you?

"Would you be able to have Spike for a while – just until I can make other arrangements? It won't be for a few weeks though, as I've got some things to sort out' I gave the obligatory, theatrical pause, then said,

"Oh, go on then, we'll force ourselves!!"

Christmas was coming in April for us this year!!

April 15th was Jake's first birthday; it was also the day that Spike came back to live with us. Chris and Sarah brought him up; it was lovely to see them again. Iain wondered if I was going to throw a party for the dogs – I usually find that a quick shot of the 'Death Stare' is retribution for facetious remarks; works every time! I had however, bought a few new toys for Jake – Staffy toys never last long. His latest favourite toy was a rope tuggy, (Winnie the Pooh was well and truly dead) which he would play with until there wasn't much left. He would then cart it around, the last few strands dangling from his mouth, until they were so minging, no one wanted to touch them. Now, he would have Spike to play tuggy with, they'd keep each other amused. I cooked some chicken for them as a birthday treat. It disappeared fairly quickly, so I'm guessing they enjoyed it!

Tuggy Time

We were absolutely delighted to have Spike back with us, but on the understanding, he was still Chris' dog, and we were just taking care of him. Yeah! Good luck with that!

Jake seemed pleased to have Spike back too, and very soon they would become inseparable. Spike had all four paws well and truly under the table!

It made me feel a lot happier the times I had to leave Jake, who always climbed onto my dressing table to watch us leave. Whenever we went out, we could see him there staring through the window, and when we came back, he would still be there. When we opened the back door, Spike would be jumping up and down, so excited that we were back, whereas Jake would come down the stairs when he was good and ready! Then, after a quick sniff to check we hadn't been cavorting with any other dogs – it was time to play! We were getting through a fair amount of tuggies; we would buy them – they would destroy them! After a while, they played together with these tuggys – one at each end. The strength they had was amazing, even though Jake was still a pup, he wouldn't give in. They looked so funny, we called them the Snout-Jousters!

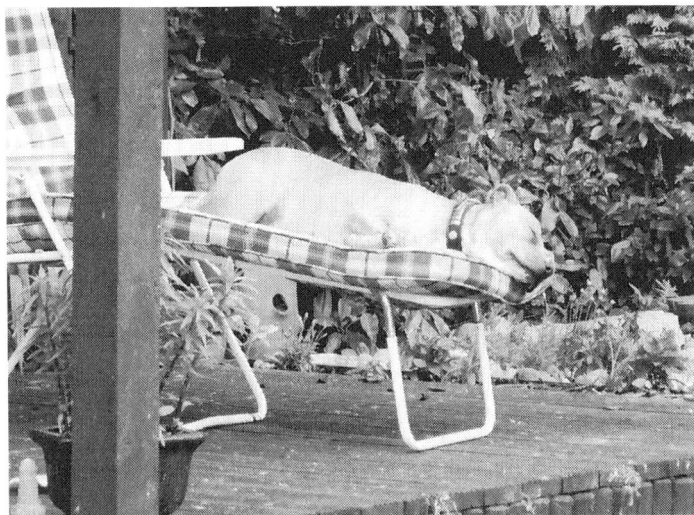

Afternoon nap.

The difference between them was comical. Hard to explain really; Think Afternoon Tea, and Donor Kebab! Jake seemed a little bit more refined than Spike. He wouldn't run if he could walk, loved a fuss, and was happy to watch the world go by from the comfort of the sofa, dressing table, or in the conservatory in Sloth- mode! He didn't like to exert himself, unless it was absolutely necessary! Iain called him 'mummy's special little soldier!'

Spike, on the other hand would have a fuss, but strictly on his own terms. He was always in the thick of things, whatever those 'things' happened to be. He was first in the queue for everything. He would run into the kitchen, inhale his dinner, and be out again in just a few minutes. Gentleman Jake on the other hand, would just saunter in, take his time, and savour every morsel.

Summer was soon upon us, and our little routine was running like clockwork. We had bought a split lead for them, and it worked very well, except for the odd time that Spike had seen something that Jake hadn't. (SQUIRREL!) He would lunge at whatever he thought he'd seen, taking Jake and me with him. My responses improved dramatically!

After one of our walks through the fields, I noticed that Jake kept scratching himself, and even though he was more than happy to lie on his back with his legs splayed in the air, I couldn't really see anything, other than a little redness where he'd been scratching. In view of this, we decided not to go to the vets immediately, but keep an eye on it for a while, but unfortunately, we had to go the following day, after waking up to find his tummy covered in spots!

After a thorough examination, I was told that it could either be an allergy to the pollen, or the canine equivalent of acne! That's all we need, a moody, teenage canine!

The vet prescribed a course of Rilexine tablets and Hibiscrub washes. After a few days, he was all clear, and seeing as how he was spot free, and still walking through the same fields, we figured it was the latter.

No longer was he the spotty adolescent, my furry baby was now a big boy!

One lovely, summer evening, Iain suggested I go with them for a stroll, and call in the pub for a swift one on the way home. Normally, I wouldn't, but it was such a warm evening, I went with them. There seemed to be a lot of people milling around at the pub, so we stayed outside and sat on the wall.

Then the Morris dancers came…

Neither of the dogs took any notice of them, until they started dancing. Jake went into a frenzy!! It was so unexpected, we were both bewildered. Was it the jingling bells, or the banging of the sticks that was upsetting him? Could it be the singing, or a combination of everything? He barked, and barked at them, he did not like it at all. He got so upset with them, we felt obliged to leave. Even walking down the street, he kept turning round and barking, he was in a proper state. As soon as we were away from the pub, he was back to himself again. I guess, like a lot of other people, he just didn't like Morris Dancing!

Summer melted into autumn without too much trouble, but come the end of October, we were at our vets with Jake again. This time we'd noticed some blood in his urine. Tests showed that there were a few blood clots there, and the vet confirmed a urinary tract infection. Nothing to be overly worried about, and hopefully, a course of Synulox would sort it out. No sooner had we given him his first dose, he was tearing around the garden with Spike. Good old Synulox!

Come the Autumn, and Spike was still with us – not that we minded! Chris had done a lot of thinking, and finally decided that Spike would be better off with us. YEAH!!

Regrettably, Chris was in no position to fund any vet bills that Spike may incur but offered to give us what he could afford when any bills arrived. We thanked him but knew we would never take him up on the offer.

Jake and Spike

BYE BYE TERRY

Those first few years sped by with very few problems. Both Iain and I became very fit, and the two Staffies kept us on our toes. It was now 2004; Jake and Spike were now five and seven years old respectively, causing chaos on a daily basis. All was going well the first half of the year, that is, until Terry found out that the company he worked for was relocating. He could have kept his job, but the new depot would be too far away for him. He decided he needed a new job. Jake would be thrilled at having his 'Bitey Buddy' around more. He adored Terry, as he would play and tease him for hours, but little did we know that Terry's plans didn't involve staying at home!

One day in early July, Terry went out and several hours later, came back with Christopher. I should have known they were up to something, as Chris lived miles away. Being a sceptical mother, my suspicions were aroused immediately - I just knew, as we mothers' do, that I was not going like whatever it was they were going to tell me. If he had brought Christopher for moral support, it must be bad.

Terry was the first to speak. He said he had good news and not so good news. Which would I like first? The look on his face, led me to believe that there was every chance that a colourful exchange of verbal's may occur after the bad.

I opted for the good.

'I've got a new job!'

'That's wonderful news bud, well done! I'm so pleased for you. Where is it?'

'Err, well, that's where the bad news comes in. It's in Iraq.'

'Yeah yeah, nice one son, of course it is; Iraq: I didn't know they had a depot over there!'

His eyes held mine as I looked at him, and deep inside, I knew he was telling me the truth.

"You're not funny Terry!… please tell me you're kidding me!"

He looked me straight in the eye and repeated that the new job was in Iraq.

"Oh, I don't think so Terry, it's far too dangerous, people are getting killed every day, and you've had no training! You get upset at the sight of too much tomato ketchup on your chips!"

My heart sank to the depth of despair. I kept hoping that he would say "gotcha" and start laughing, but he didn't. Christopher spoke up and said he'd tried his best to talk him out of it, but his mind was made up. As I'd thought, he'd wanted Christopher with him for morale support. He thought I wouldn't kill him if Chris were there!

I told him Chris would probably help me!

Nothing we said would change his mind. He would be leaving at the end of the month. Exactly two-week's time – he'd already accepted the job!

I threatened to hide his passport; said I'd give it Jake to destroy, and the bits that Jake didn't eat – Spike would have! It made no difference. I was devastated… my mum used to say 'children break your arms when they're little and your hearts when they're grown. I was now finding out exactly what those words meant.

For the next two weeks, I really tried to be positive about it, for his sake. I didn't want him to go away with the image of a snotty nosed, wailing mother, but I so wanted him to know how much I was going to miss him. It was very, very difficult. When it comes to my boys' wellbeing, I just can't do brave. Oh, I try, I really do, but it doesn't happen. I suppose I was hoping I could change his mind, but my attempts were futile.

The night before he was due to leave, we went to bed early, we had a very early start, and a very long trek down to Heathrow, but I just couldn't sleep. I prayed to God to take care of my baby and asked anyone and everyone in the heavens above to keep him safe. I lay awake most of that night, until finally, the alarm clock announced it was time to get up.

I went through the perfunctory stages of getting ready in a daze. The dogs' barley glanced at us as we made our way to the back door. Terry paused to stroke each one of them and say goodbye. He told them he'd be back soon, and they had to look after his bid while he was away. That did it! The tears were on their way and I had to pop to the bathroom for 'a last pee break' to blow my nose. I couldn't stop thinking about the danger he was putting himself in. Men in the military have no choice, but Terry did!

I sat in the back of the car and feigned a cold to disguise the watery eyes and snotty nose. I hate crying, not because I'm unfeeling, no quite the opposite, but I look such a hideous mess afterwards – I almost scare myself!

I've always hated long goodbyes; I find the anticipation much worse than the event. For me, it's easier to just have a hug and leave. However, I just couldn't do that today. I wanted every single second I could with him, before his flight was called. Once at the airport, we went to the restaurant in search of some breakfast. Iain and Terry both tucked in to a Full English; me, I had a piece of toast, but I couldn't get that down; it was sticking in my throat. I really don't know how I managed to keep it together, especially when he was called to the gate. I thought I would burst with emotion, throw myself onto the floor, and grab his legs, but I didn't. I waved as I watched him disappear through to customs. Then I dissolved into a flood of tears....

I'd been in this position once before, when his Dad was posted on an un-accompanied tour for nine months. I was pregnant with Terry at the time and thought they wouldn't send him – but they did. This day brought back all the pain and sadness I'd felt that chilly, February morning twenty-nine years ago.

I salute all the mums, dad's wives, husbands and all family members (including dogs) who go through this anguish on a regular basis because of a loved ones' profession. You are amazing, wonderful people; an example to us all.

It was a very quiet drive home, (apart from my sniffing!) except for when a sad song came on the radio – then I'd cry all over again! I just wanted to get home and hug the four-legged babies! As we pulled up to the back gate, we could hear them barking, they were waiting for us. We could see them jumping up at the window as we reversed onto the drive, Spike looked almost airborne at one point such was his excitement at our return. Seeing their little faces made me smile, even though I didn't much feel like it – you just can't help yourself when you have a Staffy! Whenever we've been out, getting home is always slightly precarious! They will knock you off your feet if you're not careful (and sometimes even when you are!)

They seemed to know I was upset that day; although they still went crazy when I walked in, they came and snuggled beside me as soon as I sat down. After a couple of cups of tea, and lots of Staffy snuggles, I felt slightly better. I would be better still once this awful day had ended. I went to bed with two dogs – one husband – several images of my beautiful boy waving goodbye and cried myself to sleep.

Even though we'd had a bad start to the month, I was determined to get my act together, but I couldn't stop thinking about Terry. Having been a service wife for many years, I knew all too well about the dangers of a war-torn country. Although Terry wasn't in the military, he was still in danger, and that worried me to death. It seemed that every time the news came on, there were reports of deaths, devastation and destruction in Iraq. Every time the phone rang, my heart missed a beat. The dogs seemed to pick up on this and stayed close to me all the time. They were the best tonic I could possibly have had. Had it not been for my little guys, I think I would have retreated into myself, but how can you be sad when there are two crazy Staffies running around!

Despite the fact every day seemed to last a week, by the time December arrived I was feeling much happier. Christmas was on the horizon, and best of all, Terry was coming home!! Yeah!!

I was determined to make this a wonderful time for all of us, and secretly hoped, that Terry would have such a good time, he wouldn't want to go back!

2004 was one of the happiest Christmases we'd had for a long time. Christopher and Sarah came up and brought a friend of theirs – Geezer! His real name was Steve, but Chris had trouble remembering his name. So, whenever they bumped into each other, usually after a few beers, Chris would say 'there's that Geezer I was telling you about' consequently, Geezer stuck. He's one of the best friends that Chris' ever had, a lovely young man, and I'm happy to say that he's become our number 3 son. We love him to bits!

Merry Stinkmas!

We all had a wonderful, happy few days that I wish could have gone on forever. Spike was going through his routines, running himself silly and making everyone laugh! It was so tempting to say 'Bath' aloud, but after he trashed the shower curtain, we gave it a rest. In next to no time, the festivities ended, and it was time for my little chicks to leave the nest once more, and let reality take over.

2005 was just around the corner - and Iraq, yet again, was waiting for Terry.

JAKE THE PEG

Time, at last seemed to be back to normal, and a day no longer felt like a week. These two dogs were making sure that we all had plenty of exercise. One day, we were having a rough and tumble with Spike, when I noticed what looked like a little wart on his lower eyelid. He wasn't happy for me to look at it, so we took him to the vets. After a quick check up, the vet concluded he had conjunctivitis, and prescribed Fucithalmic cream for it. He would need a check-up in a week, but it would take three more tubes of eye cream before it looked better. Unfortunately, Spike's eye problems were worse than first thought.

Further tests showed he had developed an ulcerated cornea, inflammation of the cornea and dry eye. Sadly, these remained permanent inflictions, but thankfully, ones that didn't seem to affect his general well-being. We now had three lots of medication for him, which would have to be given daily for the rest of his years.

It was almost May 2005, and life was ticking along fairly well. I had had a wonderful surprise for a special birthday in February (a trip to Las Vegas) which was, quite simply amazing. Someone had told us before we went, that Las Vegas was like Blackpool on speed; Couldn't have put it better myself! I remembered thinking while we were there, that I hoped I would never be as far away from my Terry (distance wise) as what I was then.

It was an incredible experience; one I shall never forget – but we missed the Staffies. Things are never quite perfect if our little lads are not with us. After a couple of days, we both start counting down 'sleeps' till we're back with them. I know – we're sad… We joked, that had we been able to bring them with us, Spike would have spent his time dive-bombing in the pool, swigging lager from a bottle while chatting up the waitress's, whereas Jake would have been on a sunbed, with a cocktail, sunglasses and designer trunks! There is no hope for me – I really should get out more! I'm afraid this is one of my silliest traits – imagining what the dogs would say/do if they could talk. I guess they'd both have a lot to say!

Later, in the Spring, we paid a visit to Nicky, but sadly, had to leave Spike with Iain's parents as Bobby and Spike just didn't get along. No matter how hard we tried, we couldn't make them friends. It was on one of our walks with Bobby and Nicky that we noticed Jake seemed to be limping a bit. We hadn't seen him do anything to injure it, however, he and Bobby did play hard, so didn't think anything bad had happened.

By the evening, he was limping quite badly. The following morning, he was much worse, so we took him off to Nicky's vet. Nicky had used this vet for many years, so we were happy for him to check out our boy. After a lot of manipulating Jake's leg, he suspected he had a damaged kneecap, and gave him some pain relief. He suggested we take him to our own vet as soon as we got home. Meanwhile, he said he would ring them, and explain the situation.

Back home, we took the first available appointment.

After another examination, our vet said he and Nicky's vet had had a chat, and both come to the same conclusion - a Luxating Patella – the kneecap is dislocated from its normal position. If left untreated, he would become both progressively lamer, painful and probably Arthritis would set in the joint. An x-ray later confirmed this, and he would need surgery to correct it. We didn't consider leaving it for one minute – it was out of the question.

My poor baby, I hated the thought of him having to have another general anaesthetic but there was simply no alternative.

Jake had his op the following week. The good news was that we could take him home in the evening – with 'the cone' as long as we didn't let him do too much walking, and definitely no running. The running bit would not be a problem - Jake the Sloth only ran when food was involved!

We had a repeat performance of his earlier encounter with a cone - bashing into everything, but overall, he managed much better this time. He started crying when we gave him his food, and we were concerned as to why he wasn't eating it. Then we realised, the cone was too big, and he couldn't reach his grub! A little fine tuning with a pair of scissors did the trick, but we took it off the following day. He still had the same 'peel me a grape' look; we're convinced it's because he knows he gets a fuss if he looks pathetic enough! The vet had told us to do a little physio with him, which we tried to make into a game. Jake's look told us what we could do with the physio; he simply wasn't interested, although he was happy to lay there and let us manoeuvre his leg for him!

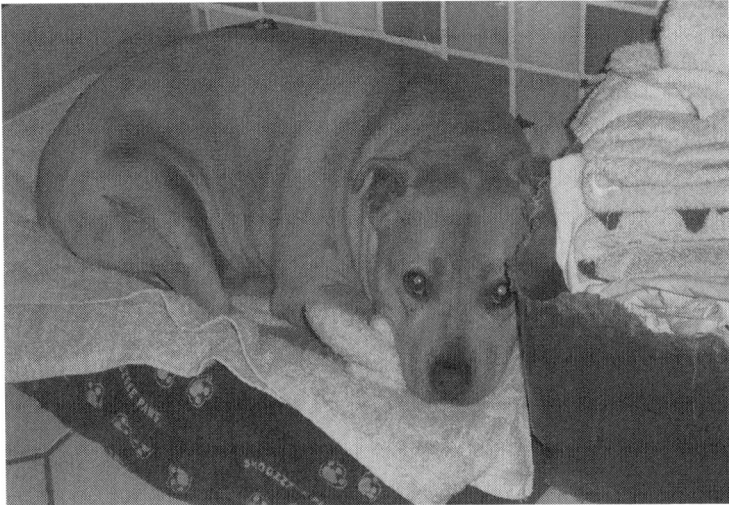

Poorly leg...

A week later we went back for his check-up. He was still quite lame but the vet wasn't overly concerned. His booster was due in two weeks' time, so we carried on with the Rimadyl until then. He seemed to struggle a lot with this condition, and it was quite a while before he was able to use it properly. However, after a few weeks, he was as good as new, and had used up all his pathetic-ness.

Summer was creeping up on us, and the weather was lovely, which seemed to promise a beautiful summer was on the way. I love the summertime; it means we can have some wonderful trips out with the boys.

It was also the time that Iain indulged in one of his passions, and bought a little Morgan, soft top sports car. I must admit, I loved it too. It was British Racing Green, with a cream and beige leather interior – a real dream car! When the weather was warm, we would leave the top off, strap the dogs in the back and take them out. They loved it!! We went here, there and everywhere! It was comical to see the faces of people in the street, when we had to stop. There was just enough room for the two of them to lie down in the back too, so they could have a snooze if they wanted to. The dogs took no notice, unless there was another dog, however, one day an unsuspecting cyclist came in for a big shock.

Have you got the keys?

We had gone to a village feat in one of the neighbouring villages, and while we were looking for somewhere to park, the dogs had fallen asleep in the back. While we were waiting at a road junction, a cyclist pulled up alongside us, and put his hand on our car to steady himself. He almost fell off, when Spike's big, white snout appeared as if from nowhere, and barked at him! He cried out and jumped off his bike. What he didn't know, was that Spike was strapped in, couldn't have got anywhere near him, and would never have hurt him.

Serves him right – he had no business holding on to our car!

The dogs never really bothered about anyone when we had to stop, unless it was another dog. Then the 'what would they say' card comes out! Without a doubt, Spike would be whistling at all the girlie dogs, whilst listening to his banging tunes on Hotdog FM (I'll put a Smell (spell) on you, and that old favourite by the amazing Tom Jones 'Stink bomb! (Sex -bomb)

Jake would be giving a look of disapproval over the top of his designer sunglasses, while humming along with his favourite song' Busy Doing Nothing', by the late, great Bing Crosby. For those of you too young to remember, (wish I was one of them) 'Busy Doing Nothing' was exactly what it said on the tin; it referred to the fact that the artist was busy trying to find lots of things **not** to do! Perfect for Jake the Sloth! (I really must get out more!)

Rutland Water is only minutes away, and we would quite often take them there. Technically, dogs are not allowed to go in, and in the past, there have been some incidents involving a particularly nasty form of algae, but as long as you keep your dogs under control and behave sensibly, people tend to turn a blind eye especially when it was very hot – and there's no algae around! Anything to do with water, Spike was first in the queue! He knew as soon as we drove down the hill, that the water was waiting for him, and he was desperate to get out. Once he was out – he was off, and very soon we would hear the inevitable splash, as he hit the water. Jake just took it all in his stride, and let Spike do all the swimming stuff!

We had a welcome visitor that summer too! Sam, our lovely Grandson, came to stay for a while. He'd met the dogs before, so he knew how hard they played. Living in Wales meant we didn't get to see much of him, so whenever we did, we made the most of it!

He loved playing with the dogs, and we loved to watch them. On one of our earlier trips out with Sam and the dogs, they had been playing with the ball on the football field. Spike got carried away with himself running after the ball and knocked poor Sam's legs from under him. It was another 'whatever you do – don't smile' times. Poor Sam sprang to his feet, and once we'd determined there were no bones broken, he was still in one piece, I had a little chuckle – only his pride was hurt! Sam tried hard to be cross with me for laughing, but he wouldn't have to wait long for payback.

Karma was in our village that day! Walking back through the fields, Sam asked me what the belt thing was on the top of the fences. He was horrified when I told him it was an electrocuted fence to keep the animals safe. I tried to reassure him it was only a very, mild charge and wouldn't hurt the animals. However, in my enthusiasm to show him what not to do, I accidentally touched it. It didn't half make me jump!

Touché Sam – who was laughing now!

After a couple of weeks, Sam had to go home again. It was always sad to see him go, as we're never sure how long it would be till the next visit. However, we'd had some fun, and made some more, lovely memories, despite the weather being somewhat chilly!

One of our favourite outings was to the seaside, so a few days after Sam had gone, we set off for the sea. We had planned to take Sam with us, but the weather was just too wet and miserable, so we had to give it a miss. Now, the weather had picked up considerably, and we packed the car and headed off. Mablethorpe is our nearest beach, but being cross country, on mostly A roads, the journey was always a couple of hours at least.

There is a huge beach there, and you can always find a vacant spot where the boys could have a good run. Spike was astounded with the sea, he couldn't get in quick enough; Jake, on the other hand wasn't too keen. You couldn't call him a swimmer; he would only go in as far as his feet would take him; he didn't like to be out of his depth. We spent many a happy hour watching Spike swim out to retrieve a ball or stick, only to see Jake pinch it off him when he came back. Why on earth would he want to risk getting his paws wet chasing a stick, when he could send his boy in for it!

It's MY stick!

Spike couldn't care less, because it meant he would just have to go in again! His plot was completely lost when he saw water - he just couldn't get enough! For some obscure reason, that only he alone knows, he wanted to drink the sea! He wouldn't entertain the nice, clean water that we'd taken for them, and no matter how we tried to stop him; he just carried on gulping. Inevitably, it always reappeared later when he yakked it back! Not wired up right!

Eventually, he would stop drinking, but by the next time we visited, he'd forgotten it would make him sick, and we'd go through the whole process again! We took balloons, balls and Frisbees with us to, which they both loved to play with, but on one occasion, Spike almost came a cropper! It was a particularly windy day, and I'd blown up this balloon, but it had blown straight out of my hand, and off across the sea. Spike lost no time in chasing it; he was off like a Polaris missile! Unfortunately, the tide was going out – and Spike was going with it!

The balloon bobbed away on the waves, and Spike followed it. We shouted him; he ignored us. We shouted some more; he ignored us some more. There was only one thing on his mind: - he was having that balloon, even if he had to swim out to France to catch it! Eventually, just as we decided to go and drag him out, he turned around and headed back. We still went out to get him, just in case he was too tired to swim. He was no lightweight, and it took both of us to carry him out, for which we were rewarded with slimy, salty, Staffy kisses – Yuk!

One day, we made the mistake of letting them off their leads at the top of the sand dunes. The main car park is on top of the sand dunes, with steps leading down to the beach. I guess we should have known better! Jake hung back, but as soon as Spike realised he was no longer tethered, he was off and away down the steps barking and scattering sand in his wake! He had no time for people sat with picnics or sand-castles, everything in his path was either destroyed, or sprayed with sand! He even had the audacity to stop and pee on someone's sand castle! I. Was. Mortified!

I suppose at this point, I should apologise to anyone who visited Mablethorpe that day, and had a picnic ruined by a noisy, high speed Staffy! It was like some kind of horror movie – I had visions of mothers picking up their children, hiding them behind their backs, or clutching them to their breasts, and running away! We caught up with the criminal and beat a hasty retreat.

Once we'd calmed him down, we decided that it might be a good idea to try another part of the beach, before we were banned from this one! We headed off down the shore, and in the blink of an eye, Spike took off like a dart, straight into the sea! We stood there quite bemused, wondering what on earth he had seen. He was on a mission for something, but what? Then we spotted it. There was a Sea Lion bobbing around in the distance. No question about it – Spike thought it was a balloon! Here we go again! We had to wade in and drag him out, because although he's a good, little swimmer, I would never take it for granted that he would be safe. After that little episode, we made sure there was always a change of clothes in the boot for us!

On the way home, they were flat out in the back of the car; stinking, farting, belching and snoring for England! It was after this trip to Mablethorpe that we noticed a little lump on Jake's paw. It didn't appear to be causing any pain, so we thought he may have grazed in the sea. Maybe he'd been bitten or stung? Hopefully it would be gone in a few days.

THE STING

As previously mentioned, we live in one of England's rural counties. Rutland is the smallest county in the U.K. and certainly one of the prettiest. Covering an area of 147 sq. miles, it has a population of around 40,000. Leicestershire, Lincolnshire, and Northamptonshire surround it. A few miles further south is Cambridgeshire, and to the north; Nottinghamshire and Derbyshire. Quite a good, central spot.

We quite liked going to new places, and there were plenty to choose from in our area. There were miles of open spaces and plenty of places for doggy walks. It was a change for us too. We'd been to the woods just over the border in Northampton with them this particular day. It was one of their favourite haunts. There are several different tracks to choose from, depending on your fitness, and how much time you have. We always went on the long walk. On the drive back home, there's a little bridge that spans a river. The river wasn't very deep at this point, so we would stop and let Spike have a dip to cool off before we went home. It was a very warm day, and strangely, for once, Jake seemed to want to go in too.

By now, Spike was off and away barking at the water, and seeing how much he could drink. Jake began wandering down to the edge, but, wanting to do his own thing, he'd wandered off in the opposite direction. He chose the wrong place to launch himself in, as further up the river it was much deeper and full of reeds. He landed in the middle of them and panicked straight away.

Before I realised what I was doing, I jumped in, fully clothed to rescue him. It came up to my waist, which was far too deep for Jake's liking – it was also felt rather chilly! Iain could see that we weren't in any danger, so when he'd stopped laughing, he helped to hoist the little lad out of the water. Thankfully, we always have lots of old doggie towels in the boot of the car, so I was able to fashion myself a very unattractive, wet, smelly sarong! (I had to dry the dogs off first!)! Poor Jake wasn't very happy. Even though it was a warm day, he was shivering!

Consequently, he was feeling very sorry for himself, and insisted on sitting on my lap on the way home. I took the opportunity to examine his paw while he was snoozing away. Was it my imagination, or was that lump looking a bit bigger? I would have to ring the vet on Monday morning.

Sunday dawned another glorious day, so we decided to make the most of it, and take them to another wood, only closer to home this time. There are several disused airfields around our area, which are now good places to doggy walk. It's kind of eerie seeing remnants of buildings, which would once have been buzzing with aircraft and people. The runways themselves are great for the dogs to have a good run – miles of open spaces, and a few old tyres knocking about, which they love to play with.

Sometimes, we would take a couple of balloons with us for them to chase and use up some of their energy. However, like everything else Spike did, he went at it full on. We had to make sure that one of us was ready to pounce on him as soon as he'd 'killed' it, as the first time he played with one, he ate it. It did re-appear the next day, as he went about his business. I noticed that his 'deposit' looked as if it was gift wrapped with the balloon. From that day on, his deposits became known as 'presents!'

After a trek around the woods, we were all ready to head home – us for a cup of tea – the dogs for their chewies and a drink. It was only about 15mins drive, so it wasn't long before we were sat in the garden with a cup of tea (and chewies!) Later, as I began to prepare dinner for us, Jake came into the kitchen to check what was on the menu. He would sit and watch me prepare food, never taking his eye off what my hands were doing. One day, I threw him a slice of carrot, to shut him up more than anything, but to my surprise, he ate it and whinged for more!!

"When did you last feed that dog?" Iain said in his teasing voice "the poor lad's so desperate he's having to eat carrots!

'He actually likes them, and I've read somewhere that they're good for him. Besides, he likes to sample the menu!'

I must confess, I do tend to spoil our dogs when I cook Sunday Lunch. I do extra vegetables for them, extra gravy and mix it with their food. It always disappears, and I'm sure it's a nice change for them. This day was no different, and after we had all eaten, we settled down for the evening to watch T.V.

There was never any room to spare on our settee when the dogs lay between us. We did have another settee, but it remained empty – they liked to be with us. When Jake landed in the middle of us, having launched himself from the rug, you just had to make a fuss, and rub his tummy, and then he'd settle down. It was whilst I was fussing him, that I noticed a lump on his tail.

'Look at this' I said to Iain 'it looks like he's been bitten or stung' I was able to feel it without causing any discomfort to him, so figured he wasn't in any pain, although, I've come to realise, that Staffies have a very high pain threshold. As one of our vets said once, "they could have a leg hanging off and only see it as a mild inconvenience!" Never a truer word spoken! However, now there were two 'lumps' in question, the call to the vet could no longer be put off – I would ring first thing in the morning.

We are very fortunate to have a wonderful group of people at our local vets, Oakham Veterinary Hospital. The Vets, nurses and the receptionists are quite simply, amazing! It's the kind of place where you could just pop in to say 'hello' if you were passing. They have the perfect balance of professionalism and friendliness, and they are never too busy to take the time to reassure or explain. When I rang, we were offered an appointment at 10.00.

I didn't mind whom we saw – they were all brilliant! When we arrived, we chatted to the ladies in the reception for a while. Jake wandered around their desk for his usual fuss, and shortly after, we were called through to one of the consulting rooms.

We found Sarah waiting for us and told her about the lumps. She examined them but was unable to throw any light as to what had caused it. She said that she would take a sample from the one on his paw to verify exactly what it was. She agreed that the lump on his tail, was possibly a bee/wasp sting, but thought had it been either of the former, he would have been in some discomfort – which he wasn't. Initially, she was hopeful that the tail lump might disappear in a couple of days, so for now, she would just take a sample from his paw.

Jake was very obliging as Sarah took the sample, (he knew there would be a chewy in it for him!) and we were soon on our way home. The vet said that she would call us with the results as soon as the lab had done their stuff. It never fails to amaze me how quickly vets can get test results, when people seem to have to wait for weeks! On our way home, I stopped and let him out for a walk. This lump certainly didn't interfere with his daily schedule, so I thought no more about it as I chased him around the fields of Rutland!

Later that day, the vet rang as promised, but I was unprepared for the news she gave me. We started off okay, then I heard the word 'cancerous' and I just didn't hear any more. I excused myself and called for Iain, who then took over the call. I felt like I was having a panic attack! I couldn't bear the thought of him having cancer – that was the last thing we expected! Poor little guy has only just got over having his leg done!

When the call ended, Iain told me what Sarah had said. The tests showed there were actually three lumps on his paw, and although the results weren't 100% conclusive, they couldn't rule out mass cell tumour, therefore, the best thing to do was to have them removed as soon as possible. It was a real shock. He was booked in for surgery the following week.

On the 24th of August, we took our little lad down to the Vet Hospital and told ring later in the afternoon to see how he was. If all went well, we should be able to bring him home that evening. We both prayed that it wasn't cancer, and if it was – it hadn't spread, and he would soon be well. I really didn't want to leave him, but I would only have been a nuisance if I'd stayed, besides that, Spike would be waiting for me, and he was bound to cheer me up. Back home, I found it hard to concentrate on anything, I was desperate to hear how he was, he was only six, and I still thought of him as – my little 'four-legged fur baby'! I couldn't believe this precious little soul had cancer, but then again, cancer has no compassion, and I found I was berating myself because of all the children and adults alike, all over the world, who are suffering from this horrendous disease. It didn't make me feel any better though...... I took Spike for a walk, and tried to take my mind off things, but try as I might, all I could think of was cancer!

When the phone call came, it was with good news. Our little lad was okay and sleeping off the anaesthetic we could collect him at six. I immediately rang Iain and the rest of the family with the good news. We went to collect him as soon as we could and waited eagerly for Sarah to bring him out.

The moment our eyes met, his little tail went in to super-wag mode! Yeah, he must be feeling better, and the sooner he was back in his own little bed, the happier he would be. We weren't out of the woods yet, we still had to wait for the test results to see if lumps were cancerous. Then, there was just the small matter of the lump on his tail...... I knew that like me, Iain would not be able to rest easy until we knew what it was. We would just have to wait for the test result.

We didn't have to wait long – September arrived, and with it, news about the lumps – it wasn't good. All three were mass cell tumours, all intermediate grade, and although they had been removed, they couldn't say that it wouldn't return. The results from his tail were bad too – another tumour. To eradicate this, he would have to have some of his tail removed. Even after this, they could not guarantee that would be the end of it. I felt the tears welling up; my poor little guy...... We booked him in for surgery the following week.

6th September dawned, and with it, that awful feeling of dread. The crazy thing was, Jake was still running about and playing as he always did, you would never have guessed there was anything wrong with him. We took him down at 8; we were getting used to this procedure. What hurt the most, was watching him walk away with the nurse, his little tail wagging. Bless him, he didn't have a clue what was waiting for him behind those doors....

It was late in the afternoon when the vet rang us. David had done the operation this time, and although everything had gone to plan, he would need to have a word with us when we got there. He could see us at six.

We went into David's room and he explained what they had done. Unfortunately, it was worse than they thought it was; consequently, he had lost most of his tail. He reiterated that although things looked fine for the immediate future, due to the nature of this cancer, it was very, very possible that it could recur. They had sent more samples for testing.

Poor Jake, I felt so very sad for him; it didn't matter to us that he had no tail, just as long as he was here with us, we would love him.

David went on to explain that Jake would be rather dozy for a while because of the medication he's had (no change there then) but he would be fine. We were to bring him back in a few days for a check-up and review. With that, he disappeared into the back to get out little lad.

It was a very wobbly, sleepy little Staffy that came through the door, but as soon as he saw us, he speeded up. The bandage where his little tail had once been, moved to and fro, but sadly, when we looked, he had no tail at all, that noxious, rotten, evil disease had taken it all. However, we still had him, tail or no tail, my boy (and his cone- we were getting quite a collection now!) was safely in my arms again, and we were going to take very, VERY good care of him!

Jakey no tail…

At home, Spike was waiting patiently for him, and went berserk when he saw our car pull up.

He was desperate to get to Jake, but we couldn't allow any Staffy shenanigans, it just wouldn't be safe, and as any Staffy owner knows, they can't play gently – they don't do gentle!

Iain put Spike in the kitchen until we had Jake settled, and then let him in. He'd put his lead on, just in case, but he needn't have bothered. It was quite lovely to see them together. It was almost as if Spike knew what had happened to his buddy. He gave him a wide berth on the floor; he didn't attempt to get in bed with him, and only gave him a **little** welcome home biff! He sniped across the floor until he was a couple of feet away from Jake, and they both settled down.

The look on Spike's face almost said 'I suppose it's grape face time again! Jake's face wasn't the problem, the main problem was going to be keeping Jake quiet. (Quiet + ~~ Staffy = absolutely not!) There was no real need for a cone for this time; he couldn't have reached back there to scratch even if he'd wanted to, so we took it off. Spike took it and destroyed it within a few minutes. I'd love to think he felt he was killing the thing that was hurting his buddy, then again…

The day after, Jake was almost back to his old self, but didn't like the bandage one little bit! We were going back to the vet in a couple of days, so he'd just have to put up with it. I had to repair it a couple of times, which didn't please him at all, but I had to make sure he kept it on.

His check-up revealed it had healed enough to leave the dressing off altogether. Jake seemed much happier without the bandage!

There was more good news to come too!

The results from his tail were back too. There was no evidence of any cancer left, it seems they had completely removed it. The prognosis was very favourable!!!

You vets' at Oakham – you're all awesome!

Even though we had the 'all clear' so to speak, we both found it very hard not to worry about him. He must have been sick and tired of me checking for lumps, I'm afraid I became a bit paranoid, but I needn't have worried, well, not for a couple of months anyway...

The only 'flies' in the ointment, were the half-wits who spoke their thoughts aloud, to let us know how horrible they thought we were to have had the dog's tail removed! I can assure you, my responses were very eloquent, but I'm afraid, not very ladylike!

We had some happy times that September too! Terry, celebrated his 30th birthday later in the month, and he decided that it would be nice to have a party at the pub in our village. He had finished his contract in Iraq and was now staying with us till his next job. I no longer had to hold my breath every time the news came on.

We invited the family down, lots of his friends, and of course – his little brother with Sarah and their close friend, Steve- Geezer to his friends (and our unofficial 3rd son) We had found many of his baby photos, enlarged them, and hung them all around the pub! However, the one that people commented about the most wasn't of Terry, it was of Jake & Spike wearing dickey bows!

We put it at the entrance, with a sign underneath saying, 'if your name's not down – you're not coming in!' To this day, I can't look at that photo without smiling, which is why I chose it for the cover.

We had a wonderful night, which carried on into the wee small hours. Terry, Chris, Sarah and Geezer all left, while Iain and I lagged behind chatting to all and sundry!

When it was time to go, we collected all the balloons that were still in one piece and took them home for Spike – that would be worth watching in the morning!

We arrived home to a rather quiet house, so we hid the balloons in the garage, and went in quietly in case they were all asleep. However, when we got in, we learned that Terry had hurt his shoulder – very badly! Geezer had brought his mini motorbike with him, and for some reason when they got home, they thought it would be good fun to do some stunts on this bike in the garden, and when it was Terry's turn, he'd fallen off! OUCH!

A trip to that A & E dept. the following day, confirmed it was a broken shoulder and he had to stay in hospital. He wouldn't forget that birthday in a hurry! Again, I could swear the dogs knew they had to be gentle with him, for neither of them even tried to jump up at him.

On returning from the hospital, it was balloon time! We shut Spike in the conservatory while we got the balloons out of the garage and tied them up around the garden. He was watching through the window, monitoring every move we made and making his 'balloon' noise (like Jake's Hedgehog noise). By the time we opened the door, he was fit to burst and looked like he was about to wet himself in anticipation. How I wish we had thought to record those few moments when he came out! He didn't know which one to kill first and ran around in circles chasing them. You could hear his jaws snapping as he lunged at them, poor Jake didn't get a look in!

He attacked every, single, one; even the ones we'd tied up on the trellises above the decking were shown no mercy. He leapt onto the garden table, then kept on jumping up till he could reach them. He then proceeded to obliterate them one by one. He was absolutely knackered when he'd finished. So were we, after all the laughing.

Halloween was the next milestone on the calendar, and with it came another vet bill. This time, Diazepam for Spike, he was absolutely terrified of fireworks. The problem was, it wasn't just for one night, these days fireworks seem to go on for weeks! Jake had also been affected; he had picked up on Spikes fear, and they were both trembling! We turned the volume on the television up, bought plug-in things that were meant to help (but didn't) and bought herbal remedies for them, but nothing seemed to work, so we had to resort to drugs. It was so sad to see this brave, fearless little Staffy dissolve to a quivering wreak the second he heard a loud bang. We can only think that it was something to do with his past....

I wish those people who seem to think it's funny to let off fireworks in the street, no matter what time of year, would be a little more considerate, if not for adults, then for the animals. Thankfully, there were no disasters that night.

The prospect of Christmas was once again at the forefront of my mind. I was really looking forward to it this year; not only was Jake back on form, we would have the full complement of babies again – both two legged and four. – Bliss!!

Sadly, my good mood wasn't to last, as a few days into December, Jake started showing signs of pain in his leg. We knew we couldn't ignore it, there was no telling what it might be, so, praying it wouldn't be what I thought it might be, I rang the vet. We had already paid a visit to the vets the week before, armed with the biggest box of chocolates we could find from Jake and Spike. We all agreed that much as we enjoyed seeing the staff, we didn't want it becoming a regular habit. That'll teach me!

We saw Andy this time, and after he'd examined Jake, he gave us his diagnosis; a Luxating patella – again, only this time in the left leg. And as a special, Christmas treat, he had another lump in his rear axilla – the hollow bit under his leg.

Merry Christmas Jake! I was despairing about these damned lumps. Why does he have to suffer again?

He would need surgery for his leg, but it could wait until the New Year. For now, I just wanted all my little chicks to enjoy themselves.

As expected, our 'festive season' was one of the best ever! The dogs went crazy – as usual, and we had to keep an eye on Spike to stop him cocking his leg on the tree – as usual! They seemed so happy to have all the people they loved together at the same time. There were lots to eat and drink, and we played Jengo – which is somewhat difficult after several alcoholic beverages!! The house was filled with laughter and love – just the way I like it!

The day after was a different story…

Chris had been winding up Spike – as per! He'd done the bath routine – chased non-existent pussycats, killed a few balloons, and he was now after the outdoor tap. Knowing he would come to no harm, we left him outside barking at it. But a few minutes later, he biffed his way through the back door, and shot through the house, soaking us all as he ran – he was wet through. How had he managed that?

The little devil must have managed to turn the tap on. Iain went out to look, and when he came back, he told us, not only had he turned the tap on, he'd eaten it too! We piled outside and stared in disbelief at what was once our outdoor tap. Such was Spike's determination to get at the water; he'd pulled the tap clean off the wall. The water was spraying everywhere!!! I know I shouldn't, but I just couldn't help but laugh. There was no way to turn it off.

Being an old house; the outside tap is connected to the pipe that supplies the road behind us. Turning off the stopcock would do nothing. Spike was overjoyed by the spring that had sprung outside his house! We were less overjoyed, and the prospect of getting a plumber out on Boxing Day didn't appeal to any of us, but there was nothing we could do.

We had to physically pick him up and lock him inside; otherwise, I think he'd have got hypothermia. He was absolutely freezing, and trembling, but he didn't seem to care. Water and balloons overruled everything! Thankfully, we were able to find an emergency plumber, and he managed to fix the tap, and for added protection, Winston, our next door neighbour covered it with a wooden box. That'll stall him!

Alas not. We never thought for one minute he would do it again, but not content with his efforts the previous day, he decided to give it another go! He had almost bitten through the wooden box surrounding it, by the time we noticed what he was doing. I quickly shooed him away and assessed the mess – bad Staffy!

Luckily, Winston, is a brilliant carpenter/handy man, and he came to assess the damage. We all decided, that we needed some serious, heavy-duty deterrents to preserve the life of the tap – wood simply wouldn't do. It is now encased in a metal tube and try as he might (and he did) he just couldn't get his teeth through it! We didn't know whether to laugh or cry; however, the plumber made the decision for us when he gave us his invoice!

HELLO 2006

On January 5th, we set off once more to take Jake to the vets for more surgery. We followed the same procedure; call in the afternoon, collect him at six. They had removed the lump from his groin area, whilst fixing his leg, and would let us know the outcome. Jake, as usual, took the whole thing in his stride. He was quite an amazing little boy really. It was simply impossible to love him anymore.

The test results came back before we were due to go for his check-up. It was a round cell tumour, but they didn't anticipate any further complications. The prognosis was looking good!

On the 16th, we were back again for a further check-up. They were pleased with how his leg was healing and said we could start building up his walks again. We were so relieved!

But by the end of the month, Jake still didn't seem to be using his leg properly, and we had to take him back to the vet. To our utter relief, there wasn't a problem, he was just scared of using it. It was then suggested that we might like to try Hydrotherapy treatment. Had that been Spike, I wouldn't have hesitated, but Jake – well, he would simply hate it. He did not like getting his hair wet!

We spoke to our insurance company, who told us, that Jake's policy covered Hydrotherapy; all we had to do now, was find a canine hydrotherapy pool! Luckily, there was a place a few miles outside Leicester, so we booked him in. Daphne offered to come and give me a hand, which I gratefully accepted. We arrived with both dogs, and the gentleman took us to the pool, and explained what would happen. No sooner had he started to speak, there was an almighty splash! Spike had broken free and landed right in the middle of the pool! I tried hard not to laugh, but that dog just had a way about him. Daphne and I were daren't look at each other, we knew we'd be hysterical in seconds!

The little pool had steps at either side, so I decided to grab him. I must admit, the water felt pretty cold to me, there was no way I was going in! Daphne shouted, 'get in ya big Jessie' but no way was I going. He came out eventually, and to add insult to injury, he shook himself all over us - we were all wet through! At that moment, I was certainly **not** amused!

Now it was time to get on with the real reason we were there. The man put a little canine life jacket on Jake and started down the steps. Jake refused to move, and you know how stubborn these Staffies can be, we just couldn't move him. He knew he would get no sympathy from me, so he made a dive for Daphne, and tried to hide between her legs. She started talking to him in a really sweet voice, and tried to persuade him into the pool, but he was having none of it. I was determined to get him in, as this would really help his leg.

Eventually, we decided that needs must, and after about 15 minutes of a battle of wits, we got him half way down the steps. Thank goodness, the owner of the place was a patient man! He'd seen dogs take a dislike to the pool but had to struggle to think of one as bad as Jake. Ironically, Spike was busting a gut to get in again! In the end, we thought that Jake might go in if Spike was in. We let Spike go in, and let go of Jake, thinking he'd follow him -wrong! The minute he was off his lead, he was off like a dart to the exit! Poorly leg or not, he didn't half get a move on!

Totally fed up with things, I decided to take them home, and have a re-think about Jake. Spike was reluctant to leave, but Jake couldn't get in the car fast enough. When Iain came home from work, he asked how Jake had gone on.

'He hated it, we just couldn't get him in. Spike enjoyed it though – we just couldn't get him out!'

After a chat with the vet, and the chap at the pool, we decided to give it another try. It's a good job Daphne was with me, for as soon as we pulled up outside, they knew what was coming! Spike couldn't get out of the car quick enough, and Jake tried to hide in the back. We had to physically carry with little devil, and almost throw him in!! He really did not like it. Spike, again, was having a whale of a time - shame he wasn't the one who needed it! After a few more attempts, we gave up. I hated seeing Jake so distressed, and although it would have been very beneficial in his recovery, I wasn't going to force him.

Overall, I think it helped Jake a bit. Not the hydrotherapy as such, but all the scuttling about trying to avoid going in the water made him use his leg fully! At our next vet appointment, the vet said it looked like the therapy had done some good. I told him what I thought, and we both had a little laugh! At least Spike had enjoyed it!

It was now March and life was ticking along nicely. I was looking forward to the clocks going forward, and the extra daylight. One morning, I noticed that Spike's eye was looking a little red. I tried to bathe it for him, but it seemed ever so tender – I didn't want to hurt him, so I popped him down to the vet. He said it looked like Conjunctivitis and gave us some more Fucithalmic cream, some liquid drops and another appointment.

If that wasn't enough, he managed to cut his leg in the groin area. He was much quieter than usual, not a term normally associated with Spike, so we told the vet at our next meeting. When the vet examined him, he said his temperature was 103 – a sure sign of an infection. He would need antibiotics along with more eye cream and drops. There would be several more trips to the vets, and it would take a couple of months before his leg was better.

As first, Spike was reluctant to let me check his leg, let alone swathe it with antibiotic cream. He wasn't as affectionate in the same way as Jake, he only did tummy rubs if he was in the mood to. He took a more direct approach, which consisted of biffs, butts and the possibility of cracked bones and bruises! However, after a few days, he didn't seem to mind me checking his groin, and thankfully, it was healing very nicely!

Spike's leg was as good as new within a couple of weeks; therefore, we were back on our usual walkie trails. One afternoon as I was rubbing Jake down after his walk, I felt another lump. This time, it was on his chest. Well, it was more like a large spot really, but by now, as I'm sure you know, I do not take any risks, no matter how small it is.

I got to the point where I thought the vet would be sick of me keep ringing up like an over-protective mother. We'd come too far to jeopardize his health by not having him checked out. So, we went to the vets, yet again for a look-see. After Jake had been given the once over, the vet thought it was better to take a sample from the lump – just in case. Fortunately, they are able to do some tests in house, and this being one of them, didn't take too long for the result. It was good news for a change, the result showed it was just debris and fat, but we had to keep an eye on it. Never mind one; I would keep both eyes on it!

When May arrived, it was time for our annual holiday to Malta. The island was beautiful this time of year; it looks greener that any other time, and all the flowers and trees are out in abundance. The temperature is easier to tolerate, not having reached its summer highs of a blast furnace! We'd been many times before and were really looking forward to it. We had first gone several years ago with Iain's sister Jacquie, and her husband Bert. We fell in love with the place, and bought a timeshare, but we've never swapped it – we go every year. We have some wonderful friends who live there, Margaret, Ray and their family. We've had some wonderful, memorable, happy times with them, we love them all.

Unfortunately, there was no-one available to look after our lads this year, so we very reluctantly resorted to kennels. We'd asked around, and a couple had been recommended, so we went along to visit them. We didn't make an appointment, as we wanted to see them when they weren't expecting visitors! We settled for one, which, although was a further away from our house, but at the time, seemed the better one.

We hated it – absolutely hated leaving them there, so much so, that I felt there was no way I was going to enjoy this holiday whilst my boys were in cages!! I know, you shouldn't use human sentiments on an animal, but I'm afraid it's just the way I'm made, and I make no apologies for it. They'd never been in kennels before, and I couldn't help but wonder what would be going through their minds? They don't love us anymore/ what did we do wrong/has she packed our chewies!!

Despite all this, we did enjoy our holiday, but rang the kennels a couple of times, just to make sure they were okay. We even sent them a post-card. (The dogs that is, not the staff!)

There are many feral cats on Malta; consequently, there are lots of postcards with pictures of cats on them. One of those would be just the job! If I had a pound for every time I've been told 'there's no hope for me' I would be a very wealthy woman! Iain wondered what the kennel staff would say when they got it. I said I hoped they would put it on their wall and tell them it was from the pack leader!

We landed back in Manchester just after lunch and after a quick coffee with Nicky, we headed off home. We wanted to get the lads from the kennels before they closed for the night.

They went completely and utterly crazy when they saw us. I think they knew we were there beforehand, as we could hear Spikes unmistakable bark in the distance. He knew we were back. They couldn't get in the car quick enough. After we had a word with the owner – who reassured us the lads had been fine, we settled the bill, and took them home.

As they were running around, reacquainting themselves with the garden, and checking out all the smells, I noticed that Spike's ear looked rather strange. It looked as if it was full of air – almost like it had been blown up. He didn't seem to mind me touching it, but I could tell it was painful. What had he done? We would have to see what it was like in the morning, and if necessary, pay yet another, visit to our vets.

That night, they slept on our bed, we couldn't bear to be apart from them, and I think the feeling was mutual. Half way through the night,

I nudged Iain to stop him from snoring, only to find it wasn't Iain – it was Spike! Bless that dog, he was well and truly chilled out, and obviously happy to be back home.

Guess what we want?

His ear looked no better in the morning, so we made an appointment for the afternoon. After a thorough check, the vet pronounced an Aural Haematoma – a blood filled pocket in his ear. We were at a loss to know how it had happened; could it be connected to something he'd done whilst in kennels? Had he hurt it in the garden? He'd only been out there for few minutes at a time. The vet said that it could have been caused by either scratching, or banging his head against something hard? Initially, the vet applied some cream and tried to drain it, but it was obviously too painful for the little man, so we made an appointment for him to be taken in and sedated.

We rang the kennels to tell them what had happened, and to see if they could throw any light on a possible cause - had anyone noticed him scratching, banging his head or noticed any kind of trauma? But they too were at a loss.

Linda A. Meredith

He had the small op the following day and was back home within hours. The vet warned us that he may need surgery again in the following months, if it didn't heal properly – we would just have to hope and wait. After a check-up the following week, it was looking good, and there were no signs of anything nasty. The cause of it however, remained a mystery....

Spike was back at the vets in June to remove a tooth that he'd broken picking up a bowling ball! One day, after a lot of grunting and groaning, he appeared with this ball that he'd found in the shed. Neither Iain or I had any idea it was there (I hazard a guess that Chris or Terry knew!) until I saw Spike with it. It was a huge, black sixteen- pound one, which I struggled to pick it up.

Spike however, didn't struggle at all, and carried it around in his mouth! He took a right shine to this ball, but goodness knows why, it was minging! Trying to get it off him was a job and half, as he wouldn't drop it until you provided something more interesting! Eventually, we hid it out of his way to stop him damaging himself – and the house! Unfortunately, it was a bit too late for his teeth; he broke one whilst 'playing' with it but losing a tooth to him was only a minor setback!

As summer reached its height, there were more trips around Rutland, and a couple to Mablethorpe. We had both learned not to take things for granted as far as the lads' health was concerned, but it seemed that every time I tried to stop worrying about him, something else would come along – and it did.

We felt another lump on Jake's leg. My heart sank, not again my little lad... I got Iain to look at it when he came home from work, and we both agreed, we needed the vet to check it out. We followed the usual rigmarole – make an appointment, go to appointment, examine dog, you know the rest...

This time, the vet wasn't overly concerned, but in view of his medical history, we ought to monitor it for a while. We were going on holiday to Cyprus with the rest of the family in October, to celebrate my brother Peter's sixtieth birthday, so, knowing the vet had said not to worry, we decided to wait until after the holiday, and try to forget about lumps, bumps, poorly eyes and ears! For a couple of weeks at least!

We took the boys back to the same kennels we'd previously used, because all the usual 'doggie-sitters' would be on holiday too! It was even worse leaving them this time, because they knew what was coming – Spike in particular was stuck to Iain's leg like glue! One of the kennel maids soon distracted him with some tasty morsels, and we made a swift exit. Sadly, we could hear him barking as we drove up the road, and we seriously considered going back for him. Had it not been for the fact that the holiday was to celebrate my brother's 60th birthday, we wouldn't have gone.

When we landed back, the first port of call was for the boys! They went crazy when they saw us; Spike's tail was in 'turbo' mode – up, down, side-to-side, round and round, it's a wonder he didn't wag himself away!

We soon had them in the car and sped off home. Jake reacts differently to Spike; after the initial 'you're back' it's like he realises that he's not very happy with us for leaving him, and sulks – or appears to. It never lasts for long though. Spike, on the other hand, just goes into overdrive and starts to malfunction!

Later that evening came a sense of 'Déjà vu.'

Spike's ear was swollen – again! Exactly the way it had swollen before, but the opposite side. Coincidence? Somehow, I didn't think so.

We booked him in for an appointment with the vet, and then rang the kennel. They could offer no explanation, where as I, well this time, I could offer a few.

The first time we said it was just one of those things, however, for it to happen again, under the very same circumstances, seemed a little more than just coincidence!

Because we could not prove that this injury had happened in their kennels, they just weren't interested. Had they offered to accept at the very least, the possibility this may have happened whilst he was in their care, it may have made a difference, but it appeared they couldn't care less!

Our vet repeated what he'd said previously - it 'highly likely' that the ear was a result of banging his head on something hard.

Like the bars on a kennel perhaps?

Another admission; another anaesthetic. They drained almost 10mls of fluid from his ear. Poor little guy, I felt so bad for him, and I felt very, very guilty. Had we not put him in those awful kennels in the first place, this would never have happened. We had done our homework, and chosen this kennel because of its location, and a verbal recommendation. We would never leave them in kennels again! However, once back home, Spike oblivious to all the fuss, and not one to let a simple operation get in his way, was out in the garden, shouting at all and sundry, before biffing me for his dinner!

Word of mouth is a very powerful advertisement; I only hope the various other dog owners we knew and told of this incident looked elsewhere to kennel their dogs! Thank God, we had pet insurance. Having said that, when we rang the insurance people this time, we discovered that our insurance will only cover one condition for one time. For example, even though they have four legs, if they break one, they will pay out, however, if he breaks another, you're on your own. This applies to every ailment and catches out a lot of people – we are two of them. Be warned, check your policy. Hopefully, things are different now.

Having got that out of the way, there was still the matter of Jake's lump. It was now November; we had watched and waited, until I was sure that it was no longer my imagination, and it really was looking bigger.

Spike wasn't faring too well either; his eye was giving him problems again however, it was the other one this time. He was scratching his ears a lot too, so off we went – again, both dogs in tow. Spike's ear wasn't really anything to worry about thankfully – it was because it was healing, as for his eye, sadly, there was nothing to be done except carry on the drops and cream; as for Jake's lump- well, it had to go!

On the 22nd, Jake had the lump removed from the right brisket area, which was sent to histology. We had a few worrying days until the results were back, but when they came, we heaved a sigh of relief. It was non-malignant tumour of the skin. We'll take that! They said we should monitor the area though, as it had the potential to become diseased in the future. They needn't worry about that – by now, I was a black-belt when it came to keeping an eye on my furry boys.

Christmas came and went without any lumps, bumps, eaten taps, broken teeth, major disasters or other misdemeanours The kids arrived, ate us out of house and home, wound up the dogs, then left. It wasn't a white Christmas, but I didn't care. I had my little fur-boys safe, sound and as healthy as could be expected. We hosted the annual 'find a square inch of carpet' game and made the most of our time together. As 2006 drew to a close, I couldn't help but wonder what the coming year would bring for us, especially my little Jake. I hoped and prayed it would be better for all of us.

Saint Francis must be getting proper sick of me!

ANOTHER YEAR BEGINS

2007 began bitterly cold and frosty. Everywhere looked white and sparkly, but despite the cold, the dogs still needed to go out. Spike couldn't care less what the weather was like, rain or snow he wanted to be out in it. In stark contrast Jake was a fair-weather dog. He didn't like the cold at all and would try and hide at walkies time! Because of the severe frost the night before, I decided on just a quick run around the field, and back home the long way, just a chance for them to stretch their legs today. I'm always reminded of my lovely old mum when I see the ice. She was paranoid about falling and would cover her shoes with old socks to steady her. My dad used to say just the sight of ice through the window, was enough for her to slip over! She certainly avoided going out unless she absolutely had to! Bless her – how I miss her...

At the far end of our village, there's a very large field, which belongs to one of the local farmers. At that time, everyone used to walk dogs around it, as it was safe, secure and the dogs could have a good run. A huge hedge lay between the field and the road. When it rained, all the water from the adjacent football pitch and surrounding fields drained into this one; consequently, it was like a little lake, except for today – when it resembled a little skating rink! We called it Lake Jake – ironic really, as Jake didn't like the water, but it rhymed with his name!

Once through the gate, I let them off their leads, and off they went. Spike immediately headed for the 'lake' not realising the effect the frozen water would have on him. It didn't bother him, he just slid to the other side. However, Jake had never experienced ice like this before. After a good sniff, he tentatively ventured out. Spike was over the other side, barking his head off, as if he was telling Jake to stop being a wuss and get on with it! Poor little guy hadn't a clue what was going on with his legs! All four of them legs headed off in different directions! He was struggling to stay upright, but within seconds, he was on his tummy, sliding along the ice. I must confess, he gave me a good laugh. He reminded me of the bit in Bambi, where as a new-born he can't stand up. Spike was thoroughly enjoying himself, I half expected him to perform a triple Salchow at the end of his performance! I was guaranteed a daily laugh with the dynamic duo!

Snow dogs

We managed to get through the first couple of months in 2007, without taking Jake to the vets, except for his booster – Yeah! Spike however, needed to have another tooth out in February, but no bowling balls were injured on this occasion! For a time, I'd tried to clean his teeth, a process he found highly amusing! He saw it as a game – one that he won every time. I gave up after a while, I was fed up of him eating the toothbrushes!

As Spring approached, the weather improved, and I was out and about with the dogs. Daphne would come with me sometimes. She lived in the next village, which was also en route to one of their walks, so we would pick her up on the way. One of these trips will be forever engraved in my mind, as we both ended up in fits of laughter thanks to Spike.

We had driven out to Clipsham, well known for its topiary avenue of Yew Trees. It was once the carriage drive to Clipsham Hall, which lies at the end, and claims to have 150 shaped Yew Trees that are said to be 200 years old! Most have been clipped in the shape of animals, others to commemorate important, historical events. All this, of course meant nothing to Spike. He showed no respect as he cocked his leg against them. It must have seemed like heaven to him; all these trees lined up just waiting for him to christen them! I wouldn't mind betting, that he peed on every one of them at some time!

Behind the Yew Trees, there's a trek that winds through another, larger woods. The dogs just loved racing through the trees sniffing everything in sight! Having walked a fair way down the back path, both Daphne and I felt the call of nature – we both needed the loo! As you would imagine, there were no facilities in the woods, but plenty of tree coverage, and when needs must…

The dogs were running around chasing each other, and there was not another soul in sight. I disappeared into some bushes, and when I came out, it was Daphne's turn. I shouted for the dogs to come back, and Jake appeared almost immediately. I couldn't see Spike, but just as I was about to call him, I heard a very loud shriek! It was Daphne shouting from the bushes, 'get out of it you silly bugger!' and within seconds, Spike came running towards me, Daphne appeared shortly after.

'That dog nearly knocked me flying – sticking his snout where it shouldn't ought to be! There I was, minding my own business, when a wet nose came at me from behind, poked me in the bum, and almost knocked me flying!'

I started to laugh, and the more I thought about it, the more I laughed.

'Poor Spike' I said.

'What d'you mean poor Spike; what about me?'

'Well you're okay, but the repercussions for that little lad could last the rest of his life – he could be traumatised!'

'I'll give you traumatised when I get hold of you; You're not too old for a good-hiding!'

Fortunately, I could run a lot faster than Daphne!

I've dined out on that story many times since that day!

With so many places to choose from for out walkies, we're never at a loss for a change of scenery. There's a pretty little village called Kings Cliffe in Northamptonshire. Willow Brook, is a tributary of the River Nene, and runs through the pretty, little village. There are places to cross the brook, but our favourite crossing place was the Ford, which the lads just loved. Even Jake was happy, as he could walk across without getting his hair too wet! I used to go in with them too if it was warm!

Jake really surprised us one day, after I'd thrown a stone in the water for him. He chased after it, dipped his head in the water, and brought back the same stone! With the hundreds of stones around there, it seemed improbable that he had found the same one, so, thinking it was just a fluke, I threw another.

The same thing happened, in fact, it happened again and again!! each time, he brought back the same stone. This little water-shy dog had maybe been kidding us on all along! Another time we arrived, to find the kids had fashioned a swing from some rope and a large tyre. It was tied up to a huge branch that overhung the river. As soon as Spike saw it, he had to have it! The bit of the brook where they play isn't particularly deep at all, but where the swing was, was well out of Spikes depth! A mere inconvenience to him! What he did next just illustrated how strong/determined this dog was.

He was swimming up-stream towards the tyre, and suddenly sprang from the water in an attempt to grab it! We heard the 'snap' of his jaws as he missed it – but he wouldn't miss it again. the next time he hit his target, and using nothing but his teeth, swung on it in mid-air!! I could do nothing but laugh, he looked so funny. Silly Staffy, I'm sure I could write an entire book just about his capers!

It was almost time for our trip to Malta, we were both looking forward to a well-earned rest, but the prospect of leaving the boys just took the cherry from the top. How sad are we...

This year, Chris and Sarah were going to look after the dogs for us, down at their house in Milton Keynes. The dogs loved them both, as Chris played with them, and Sarah spoiled them. It was a bit of a trek driving down there, and then back up to Manchester for the flight, but it was worth it to know that they would be well looked after, and not locked up! There were some lovely walks around their area, and it was quite close to the Grand Union Canal. Spike would LOVE it!

As always, the two weeks were over far too quickly, and soon we were boarding the aircraft back to Manchester. It was only a matter of time before we would be covered in Staffy kisses – and we couldn't wait!! Having family there is great; not only do we get a lift to the airport, courtesy of Nicky, but we are able to leave the car at her house too! Bless her, she's one of the sweetest, kindest people I know, and we both love her to bits!

We'd spoken to Chris and Sarah a couple of times during our holiday, and been reassured that everyone was okay, both two legged and four!

The journey down to Milton Keynes seemed to take forever, as it always does when you can't wait to be somewhere! When we finally pulled up outside their house, we couldn't resist winding the dogs up by knocking on the window. They went ballistic! Once the door was open, they lunged at us, sniffed us to within an inch of our lives, then Spike went and stood by the car – his way of telling us, - just in case we harboured any thoughts of leaving him behind, he was ready to go home.

Sarah said there hadn't been any problems, but then Chris told us about the incident with the cat-flap, which had us in fits of laughter.

They had a beautiful, white pussycat called Fluffy, which Sarah's mum was looking after so they could have the dogs, for which we were very grateful. But having a cat meant they also had a cat-flap.

It appears that one of the times Spike wanted to go out, they didn't respond fast enough to his request, so he tried to shove his big, white head out through the cat-flap! He tried to biff his way out but got his big, meat-head stuck and couldn't move. They tried all kinds of things to get him out to no avail, so eventually, Chris had to remove the cat-flap, with his head still in it! It could only happen to Spike! This story has been a constant source of amusement ever since and earned him yet another nickname...... Meat'ead!

So apart from a broken cat-flap, everything was fine. I only wish we could have seen it!

Things were going tickity- boo that year, the family were all in fine fettle, and there were no health issues with the dogs - Just the way I liked it.

It wasn't to last....

Mid-summer, Spike began to show signs of pain in his front leg/shoulder. The way he plays, I'm not surprised! The vet suspected Arthritis and told us he had to rest for 10 days, during which, he should be kept on his lead, and only out for fifteen minutes at the most. Ten days! The vet obviously didn't realise who he was dealing with. We can't even get him to rest for ten minutes, never mind ten days! The only chance of achieving this, would be with a straight jacket and some sedatives! We tried our best to keep him 'quiet' but it wasn't easy, especially when it was walky time. He was not impressed with this idea, he was desperate to run and play with Jake, but we kept his lead firmly on.

At his check-up two weeks later, the vet saw signs of improvement, but told us that shoulder injuries can often take a long time to heal. We could now start to let him off his lead for a few minutes, gradually lengthening the time each day for another two weeks... He was ten years old by now, but showed absolutely no sign of slowing down, but the Arthritis would force him to eventually.

As the leaves began to reveal their magnificent, Autumn kaleidoscope of colour, Spike was back at the vets again, this time, it was because he had a few lumps between his toes. The vet lanced them and drained some pus and told us to rest him. They said it was probably an infection after treading on something. Rest him they said. (We know how Spike feels about resting) He didn't think there'd be any problem e.g. of the cancer type, after a couple of weeks of Rimadyl and salt water washes, he was confident he would be as good as new, and thankfully, he was. Sadly, old age was beginning to catch up with our old boy...

Jake wasn't faring too well either. I thought I could feel a couple of lumps again, this time in his little 'boy bits' Now, being completely paranoid, I was beginning to wonder if I was finding phantom lumps! A couple of days on, and we were both in agreement; there was nothing phantom about these latest ones! We'd thought it too good to be true that Jake's health had been good for the most part of the year. Off we went – again!

I wasn't surprised to learn that he would have to have these lumps removed, the sooner the better. We made the arrangements for November 5th – hopefully, come the evening, he would be too woozy from the anaesthetic to be worried about fireworks!

I left him with the vet, and went to do a little shopping, before going home to take Spike for his walk. As I was opening the door on our return, I could hear the phone ringing, but by the time I'd got in it had stopped. I gave it a couple of minutes, then listened for a message.

There was one – and it was from the vet; could we ring immediately.

My heart dropped to the floor, as I imagined the news they might be about to give me. I really didn't want to make that call, at that moment, everything was fine, and if I didn't make the call, it would stay that way. If only...

I dialled the number and waited...

After a few moments, I was speaking to Heather, one of the many lovely receptionists there. I held my breath as she put me through to David, who'd done the procedure. He explained, that whist preparing Jake for his surgery, they had found another lump, and they needed to check that they could remove it.

I exhaled, and told him yes, absolutely, get rid of anything that shouldn't be there! In one way, I was relieved to hear that my lad was okay but saddened to hear they'd found another lump. I would take it for him if I could...

So, besides the ones we'd found on his penis, there was one in his chest, and another one in what I would call his armpit on his front leg. I was beside myself – beyond crying. Yet again, looked to the sky, and asked why? Why does this keep happening to my little guy?

Although we'd become proficient at waiting for test results, the anxiety seemed to get worse. When they rang with the results, they were as good as we could hope for. Two Lipomas, and one mast cell – all removed successfully. A week later, we were told that the samples they had taken showed no evidence of cancer. Thank you (again) Saint Francis!

Ten days later, we popped back for his final check-up – only to discover another lump behind his triceps. I'm amazed how fast these lumps appear! By now, we knew the procedure like clockwork; Another sedation to acquire a sample, then wait for the results. I don't know how much more of this my little guy can take – or us for that matter, then I figured if Jake could be strong, then there was no question - we absolutely must be too! The results showed nothing nasty, but because it was Jake we would need to keep an eye on it. Will this ever end? I think I knew the answer to that question – I just wasn't ready to face it yet...

The end of the year was approaching fast, and this year would be pretty much a repetition of past ones; Boys and partners turn up-eat/drink me out of house and home – torment the dogs – then leave! This year, there was another thing that Spike took a shine to – shine being the key word!

Spike had always liked chasing things that were not actually there i.e. reflections. Using a mirror is a good one, and having discovered this many years before, poor old Spike has been teased unmercifully with my make-up mirror. However, this year, Chris had brought with him one of those laser pens to show us. In all fairness, none of us realised what effect it would have on Spike, but it was up there with water and balloons! He almost went into orbit when he saw it!

Once Chris saw the effect it had on Spike, there was no stopping him! Anyone seeing his performance that evening, would completely understand why we say that Spike isn't wired up right! We would definitely need to reset his circuit breakers after this! Bless that silly, daft, crazy, mad, loopy and utterly wonderful dog! I'm surprised he had the energy to go for his walk after.

We also found that he was more than interested in the light on Terry's watch, which Terry just had to exploit! The pen and the watch put him in 'meltdown mode' the poor dog didn't know if he was coming or going!

Jake watched on from the comfort of the sofa, he had better things to do than get involved in Spikes frivolities. He had sleep to catch up on, so he settled down for forty winks – and a good stink! Two thousand and eight was almost upon us, and we all wondered how many months we could get through without having to visit the vet!

My little guy...

HERE WE GO AGAIN!

The year began much the same as any other. The weather was reasonably mild considering it was mid-winter, and we managed to get through six weeks without a trip to the vet! They both had to go early February, as one of them, had been very ill during the night. Having two means that you can never be 100% certain who did what, so they both had to go. Jake for once didn't seem too bad, but the vet didn't need a stethoscope to listen to Spike's tummy – we could all hear it gurgling away! This, we were told goes by the rather fancy name of Borborygmi – the sound the gas makes when it's gurgling through the intestines. And if it was in there – it had to come out! This... could get messy!

Its cause can simply be the result of hunger, a change in diet, or something they've picked up and eaten outside which they shouldn't have! That'll be number three then! However, it can also be a symptom of other, not so quick to fix things, one of which is inflammatory bowel disease, especially if accompanied by sickness and/or diarrhoea, so it's always best to check. The vet suggested we starve him for a while (he wouldn't like that!) and then feed him a little chicken (he would approve of that) for a couple of days.

Thankfully, it did the trick, and he was soon back to his usual 'eating for England' self. Sadly, I thought he looked a little lame, looked as though he may have trodden on something? I would keep my eye on it, but somehow, I knew it was going to involve another trip to the vets.

Sure enough, as the days passed, it seemed to get a little worse, so we made an appointment. The vet suspected the Arthritis could be getting worse but wanted to do tests to confirm. Within days, he had had tests, x-rays and a diagnosis! The results showed he had Osteophytes (little ridges found in the area where the cartilage has begun to disintegrate) in both of his shoulder joints. That, along with his Arthritis was going to cause him pain, so the vet prescribed some anti-inflammatories and some flex-chews.

Our poor little guy was going to need this medication for the rest of his life. For the moment, he couldn't care less, as he bounced out of the room. Like us humans, once he got going, he could move better. The vet said he needed to rest – good luck with that; he doesn't do rest, I'd just have to keep him on his lead for the foreseeable.

This wasn't as hard as I'd expected. I think he knew his puppy days were gone. He was almost eleven now, and all the years of running amok, swimming for England, performing ice-skating manoeuvres, chasing shiny things and swinging from tractor tyres were behind him. Didn't stop him trying though! Whenever I was able to let him off his lead, he was off and away as usual – but ready to go home a lot sooner.

A strange thing happened that summer too. It happened when Daphne, popped in for a cuppa, and to swear at me. The dogs always went mad when they saw her, she loved them to bits. Although she'd never admit it, she had a bit of a soft spot for Spike, and it seemed the feeling was mutual. However, this day he wouldn't go anywhere near her. Neither of us could understand why, but Daphne, as usual, had her own ideas. Jokingly, I said it was because he was sick of her – she put it in simple terms – "He's just being a pain in the arse – most males are!" meanwhile Jake soaked up all the attention on offer, he'd have Spike's share too!

As soon as she'd gone, he appeared again, as though nothing had happened, but the very next time she came, he was off like a shot! This time he ran upstairs to get away from her! I knew she was upset; I was too. We just couldn't figure out what his problem was, however, this would be revealed later in the year.

Jake had gone almost a year without any trips to the vets, except of course, for his annual injections. Life was becoming – dare I say – a little 'hum drum'! As always, just when I think everything's fine – boom! This day, we'd taken a ball up to the football field, and they were having fun chasing it around. Jake decided it was 'doggy-do' time and headed off towards the surrounding shrubs.

I noticed that he seemed to be taking rather longer than usual, and I found him straining to relive himself; Several times he squatted but was unable to pass anything. As we walked home, he made several more attempts, but nothing was happening. I would have to ring the vet for some advice. Their advice was to take him in.

While I was driving there, I remembered something that could explain his predicament. The day before, I had cooked a Leg of Lamb for lunch, and the bone had been put in the bin – or so we thought, until we saw Jake eating it! The outside bin was full, so the liner containing the bone had been put by its side, ready to go in when the bin was emptied the following day. The pair of them had had a go at it, and it seems Jake was the victor!

We took it off him, which he wasn't too thrilled about it, but we didn't allow them bones. I wondered if this was the reason why he couldn't 'go'?

There were no visible signs to justify his discomfort, so the vet gave him an enema to see if that would do the trick. Although it enabled him to 'go' it was quite obvious he was in pain, and in view of what we had told the vet about the lamb bone, he felt he should examine him under sedation.

While this was taking place, I popped to see Iain's parents, and told them about his latest malaise. They always took an interest in the boys' welfare and were saddened to hear that their 'Grand-Doggie' was at the vets – yet again! I went back to collect him and found out what the problem was - he had Colitis. It was nothing to worry about, and easily treated. He had, however, found, what he described as a 'knobbly mass' under his back leg, which they'd had a look at. Further investigation would show it was just a 'fatty mass' and (hopefully) nothing to worry about! We'll take that!

Not long after that episode, I received a very distressing phone call from Claire – Daphne's daughter, to tell me that Daphne had been taken into hospital; she was a very poorly lady. The had done numerous tests, which alas, confirmed she had cancer. Sadly, they had been told to prepare themselves for the worst. I knew she'd said she didn't feel too good, but none of us were expecting that news! Daphne wasn't one for being poorly, she's a bit like a Staffy – hard as nails!

There was nothing to it, I would have to go and be extra rude to her every chance I got! Daphne didn't do hugs, or gentle stuff. Her terms of endearment, consisted of calling me rude names, which, I might add, were thrown straight back at her! That was just our crazy way. Had anybody heard us, they would never believe we were the best of friends.

Halloween was creeping up again, and although my boys are grown up, I love to see the little ones when they come 'Trick of Treating'. One of the busiest nights of the year for the dogs – they love it! They barked at every knock on the door and sized up the strange looking little people on the doorstep! Unfortunately, as soon as they heard a bang, they fled back inside. Which reminded me to get some Diazepam tablets for the dreaded Bonfire night!

It wasn't to be just Diazepam that I needed though, for I had noticed another lump on Jakes ear....... I'm absolutely astounded at how quickly these damned lumps appear!!! It would need to be checked out, and this time, we would have several days of worrying, as the sample had to go to an outside laboratory. My heart was filled with dread at the possibilities, that I just couldn't bear to think about....

The results came back on the sixteenth of December. The lump was a Mast Cell Tumour, and the tests suggested that it was intermediate to high grade. It would need to be removed, and the vet also advised us, that Jake may need to be referred to a vet school or the like, for removal and Chemo if necessary because of the nature of this tumour.

By now, we had run out of insurance cover, as they will not pay out for the same type of cancer twice. Not in the policy we had anyway.

We trusted our vet implicitly and would follow their advice to the letter. After a lot of discussion between the various vets and the veterinary college, it was decided that our vet at Oakham would carry our Jakes operation. We were both relieved to hear this, we could think about referrals later down the line if necessary. He was admitted on the eighteenth of December to have it removed. While the vet was performing the op, he noticed another Mass Cell Tumour under his elbow, so they removed that as well. I tried to keep positive, by joking that he could do with losing a little weight, but inside, my heart was breaking. Deep down, I knew it was only a matter of time...

When Iain and I went to collect Jake, the vet was asking how Spike was; I told him he was ok, but was acting very strange around a family friend that he'd known for years, who was now in hospital (Daphne's cats also saw this vet, so the vet knew her) He asked what was wrong with her, and when I said cancer, he explained that sometimes animals can smell it on a person, and maybe that's why he ran away? He would know it was an unfamiliar smell and wouldn't like it. It never ceases to amaze me how clever dogs are.

It made perfect sense – Spike had known before any of us that something was wrong with his buddy. If only he could have told us.

On the journey home, I snuggled Jake in the back seat of the car. I told him how very sorry we were to keep putting him through this, and how much we loved him. His response was a lick across the face. He doesn't hate me after all!

Christmas was a very solemn one that year. Both Terry and Christopher came home, but we were all feeling a bit down. None of us particularly felt like celebrating, even the dogs were quieter than usual. They still had their parcels to kill – which they did unmercifully, but there was a little spark missing. We were all worried about Daphne and Jakes cancer returning. Still, we tried to make the best of things; we ate, drank and watched far too much television. Mostly, we spoiled the dogs with lots of cuddles! I hoped and prayed with all my heart, the new year would be kinder to both Daphne and our little four-legged boys!

At Jake's check-up at the end of the month, the vet told us that it was highly likely the cancer would return. We could only hope and pray that it wouldn't. It seemed to me, that God was taking Jake to 'The Bridge' a little bit at a time. It seemed pointless to wish for a Happy New Year...

Bah humbug!

DIFFERENT YEAR, SAME PROBLEMS

It was a solemn start to the New Year, I made a mental note NEVER to say, 'it can't be as bad as the one just gone' because invariably, it could, and quite possibly would! January's always a busy month for us, and that one was no exception. The dogs were as well as could be expected, but I was scrutinising Jake at every opportunity. Fortunately, he didn't mind rolling on the floor with his legs in the air; it made my inspections much easier.

Towards the end of February, a little spot appeared on the side of Jakes nose. I wasn't overly concerned, as it was quite literally a spot – but it still needed an eye keeping on it. The end of the month brought shattering news for us all. Daphne, my crazy, amazing, wonderful friend, had passed away during the night. We were all absolutely shattered. I was fortunate enough to have this wonderful lady in my life for many years.

She was one of the blessings in my life, a true, sincere friend. Without a shadow of a doubt, I knew my life wouldn't be the same without her. She was my mum, big sister and best mate all in one. Who else would cuss me like she did? Ironically, her funeral was held just a few days after what would have been her sixty ninth birthday.

Mid-March, Jake's little spot looked somewhat bigger, so off we went again. Tests were taken, as per usual, and we would just have to wait for the results. Thankfully, they found nothing nasty. Yeah!!!! We love that! The vet gave us some Fuciderm cream and sent us home. Good result!

Between March and July, we visited the vets' several times with one or the other of the boys. Jake was getting one thing after another. He had a sore ear, a nasty, allergic rash round his little 'boy bits' and Rhinitis. We were spending so much time with the vets, I felt they'd be giving us our own door-key and an invite to the office party before much longer!

We got to the summer, without anything untoward happening, and as the summer was so warm, we decided to buy another paddling pool for the dogs; or should I say Spike? He'd eaten the last couple we'd bought. The weather was really hot, and this would be a great way to keep them cool. I didn't want to pay too much, on the other hand, I wanted it to live for more than a couple of hours! I eventually found an inexpensive one and came up with (what I considered to be) a very good idea! I placed the pool under one of the trees in the garden, then tied the hose to a branch in the tree – a very high branch in the tree! It had to be out of range of snapping jaws!

Spike-loved-it; he was beside himself!

Mind you, we had to be extremely careful where Spike and hosepipes where concerned; the tricky little Staffy would be overcome with a crazed enthusiasm at the mere hint of a hose pipe! We had a thirty metre one when Spike first arrived, but having to keep chopping bits off, and bodging it up where he'd bitten it, it was around 10. We must have bought at least half a dozen sprinklers and connectors too – he was a demon!

Water, as usual surpassed all his other little 'Spike-isms!' So much so, the only way to get him out was to drain the darn thing with him in it! Jake wouldn't go in, of course, but I found that if I put his beloved red ball in there, he'd venture in to get it. Obviously, if he could get Spike to get it for him, he would, but sometimes he just had to get his paws wet. They gave us several hours of hilarious entertainment that summer, an absolute joy to watch! A bit like children, come the evening and they'd be flat out!

There were a couple of trips to the seaside, and although they seemed to enjoy themselves, they took things a lot slower. Despite his somewhat leisurely pace, Spike even managed chase a seagull when it came a bit too close. He could still 'see 'em off!' if he wanted! Jake, as usual, left the all things requiring physical exertion to Spike. I dared to let myself believe that we just might have seen the last of the cancer...

It was a very quiet Christmas that year; Terry was living in Egypt, he'd got a job as a Diving Instructor, and having a whale of a time. Unfortunately, it wasn't a very well-paid job, so he wasn't able to come home for Christmas. Chris was still in Milton Keynes and was spending the time with Sarah's family for a change. I'd had them here so many times, I wasn't going to complain. Iain's parents came for lunch, but it was much quieter than the usual uprising!

Somehow, I felt this was a sign of things to come.

POORLY SPIKE

February 2010.

Spike seemed to be off his food, which wasn't like him at all. He seemed to be listless, but there were no visible signs as to why. I decided to follow him into the garden to check that his little doggie bits were in working order. Sure enough, the answer lay right there – there was blood in his poo. Not wanting to panic too much, I thought we'd wait until morning to see how he was. He had a peaceful night, but when he went into the garden that morning, his little legs just seemed to give way. We called the vets immediately.

Luke was on duty and gave Spike a thorough examination. He wanted to do some blood tests, which would take time, so suggested that we leave him there for the time being. There were several things that could be causing it, but we tried to focus on the less serious ones. We left him in the very capable hands of our vet and went back home to Jake.

Later that afternoon, Luke called us with the news. Spike had had a gut bleed; possibly caused by the NSAIDS he'd been taking, after all, he'd been on them for quite some time. An ultrasound scan had shown no obvious tumours, he couldn't guarantee things would stay that way. He was very anaemic and may need a blood transfusion at a later date. This would be very beneficial for him, but for now, we would try iron tablets for a few days, and make a decision later. It had never occurred to me that there was such a thing as blood transfusions for dogs, but there are several pet blood banks around the country. They, together with generosity of some amazing dog owners, have saved the lives of hundreds of dogs. Bless every one of you; you're all wonderful people!

Spike's check-up was scheduled for Monday afternoon, which had given him roughly 48 hours on the iron tablets. Iain and I had decided to go ahead with the transfusion if the vet recommended it. The vet had a good look at him, and said that although there was a slight improvement, the transfusion would do him the world of good, almost like a booster. We agreed and made arrangements for the procedure.

I believe the blood came from the Pet Blood Bank at Loughborough, Leicester (thank you guys!) and was with our vets first thing the following day.

It didn't take very long to administer the blood, just about three hours, but he to be constantly monitored. We could bring him home that evening, with his own special cocktail of drugs. His re-check would be in a week's time.

The benefits were almost immediate, as the following day he was practically 100% Spike again. We were absolutely delighted. It was almost as if he'd been given a magic potion!

The following week, at his check-up and the vet was very pleased with him. His appetite had returned, his presents no longer contained blood, and he was trotting up and down the stairs again. More importantly, his tail was back at optimum velocity - full speed wag! He would still need to take iron tablets every day, but that was a small price to pay to have our crazy Spike back his old self. Turbo tail was better!

In April, I left Spike with Iain, and took Jake up to visit Nicky. It was lovely to see Jake and Bobby together again, but something wasn't quite right. The only way to describe it, is to say Jake had lost his 'mojo!'

He'd growled at me a couple of times, when I'd tried to get him to do something, and just seemed really grumpy. This wasn't like him at all. He had never, ever growled at a person, least of all me! At one point, I was convinced he'd fallen down the stairs. I heard him go up, and thought he was going to bed, but within seconds, he was back in the kitchen. He couldn't have gotten down that quickly, surely? I would keep my eye on things and see how he went. Fortunately, there wasn't a lump in sight! I prayed it wasn't a prelude of something to come, but we could never say never where Jake's health was concerned.

Back home, things seemed a little strange – I was looking at Jake, but Jake wasn't acting like Jake! He became withdrawn and tetchy; the complete opposite to his usual demeanour. He didn't seem to be in any pain, still no lumps, bumps or irritations anywhere, but something was wrong. Something was very, very wrong.

I took him to the vets, where we saw Catriona, but all I could tell her was that he seemed to have lost his mojo. She examined him, and finding nothing physically wrong with him, she suggested we just keep an eye on him. There was nothing to be done…

A MIDSUMMER
NIGHTMARE...

It was June, and summer had well and truly arrived in Rutland. We were looking forward to my seeing my sister-in-law, Janet, who was visiting us on Saturday. The evening before was a beautiful warm, summer evening. Iain had done his usual 'Friday night thing' (paid his respects to the Barflies) and we were relaxing in front of the TV, well, one of us was considerably more relaxed than the other, but we won't mention Iain's snoring! Jake hadn't wanted to go with Iain to the pub, which seemed a little strange, but it had been a warm day, so we didn't make him go. For a change, Iain was in the armchair, because Jake had taken up residence on his favourite spot on the sofa, sprawled out like a wet lettuce!

From the corner of my eye, I noticed that Jake was fidgeting a lot – "Ah, he's having puppy dreams" said Iain, but I was a little more concerned, You see, when I moved to wake him up, I realised that he wasn't sleeping at all, more alarmingly, he didn't respond to my voice; then I noticed the foam around his mouth I was really, really concerned. I stroked him and spoke softly to him – I didn't really know what else to do. Eventually, Jake calmed down and looked at me, as if to say, 'what's going on?' Iain tried to reassure me that he was just having a dream, but my heart couldn't be fooled – I wondered if he'd had a fit? I kept a very close eye on him for the next couple of hours, but nothing happened.

I was reluctant to leave him and go to bed, but I knew there was nothing I could do until the morning, so unwillingly; I headed up the stairs to bed. Sleep evaded me for hours, I was listening intently for any noise from downstairs, but heard nothing. I went down a few times to check on him, but all seemed well, so I went off to bed, and eventually, I drifted off to a restless sleep. When I awoke on Saturday morning, Iain was at my side with a cup of tea. Bless him, he brings me one every day, and try as I might to repay his kindness, he always wakes up before me!

'Jake's alright – he's been out to do doggie stuff, and he's gone back to his bed. Doesn't seem to be much wrong with him this morning. The fact that he'd gone back to bed concerned me – he always came up to me after his morning ritual.

But, I was so thankful to hear that news, maybe I was panicking over nothing after all, however, it worried me somewhat; he seemed to be spending a lot of time in his bed lately, and I was seriously afraid it may be something more significant than just being tired. He didn't make any effort to get out of his bed when he saw me, so I knelt over, and gently rubbed his ears. He seemed to approve of this!

Seeing as how he looked ok, I decided to wait and see if anything else happened through the day. I would watch him like a hawk, and if he so much as flinched in his sleep, I was calling the vet! He seemed to be alright but had taken to pacing up and down the garden, and going around in circles, and although I thought this was quite odd, I didn't think it was indicative of anything.

He walked into a corner of the garden, and just stayed there. Strange... he did this a few more times, but again, we didn't think anything of it. My sister-in-law Janet, her friend Tracey and their two lads, Jake (my nephew) and his friend Daniel, arrived Saturday morning as planned. I'd spoken to Janet earlier in the week and told her about Jake being off colour. I didn't mind them coming, but I needed her to explain to the lads, that Jake, the social butterfly, was not his usual self, and they mustn't make a fuss of him. They're lovely lads, so I knew there would be no problem. Over a coffee, I launched into the happenings of the previous night with Jake. As expected, he gave everyone a wide berth, until later, when he deigned to be stroked! We went about preparing the BBQ and catching up with events since our last meeting. Jake appeared as the food was being eaten, so I figured that perhaps there might not be anything lurking beneath the surface after all…

Later that evening, we were relaxing with a glass of wine, and having a laugh. The dogs were outside napping in the garden, and all was well in the world! Suddenly, Daniel called out.

'I think there's something wrong with Jake, look at him!'

We all dashed to the door, to see my little lad convulsing on the floor. This time, there was no mistaking, he was definitely having a fit.

Luckily, Tracey had had some experience with epilepsy, and knew immediately what to do. I, on the other hand could do no more than shake and watch. I didn't hesitate this time; I went straight to the phone and rang the vet.

I spoke to the vet on call, Vanessa, who was absolutely wonderful, she was obviously used to doggie parents ringing up in a panic! She spent ages on the phone with me, calming me down, and explaining what to do. She also mentioned a few things that could be causing the fits – all of which were horrid, but after a while, I felt more confident about what to do, and bade her goodnight. She had said to call anytime if I was at all concerned. I thanked her and rang off.

That night, we took Jake up into our bedroom to sleep that night, so that we could keep an eye on him, and be there to comfort him should he have another fit. All in all, he had another three fits throughout the night, but now, I could be of some use this time, even if it was just holding him. In the morning, we all congregated downstairs and I filled in the girls on the night's events. While we were having breakfast, Jake had another fit, so we decided to take him down to the emergency clinic they held on Sunday mornings. It was still fairly early, so I had to wait a while.

When I did ring, I was put through to the lovely lady who I'd spoken to previously. Fortunately, the vet who was treating Jake was on-call that day, so I didn't need to spend time explaining his medical history. He told us to take Jake down immediately. We didn't need telling twice.

We arrived about half an hour after the phone call, and the vet was waiting for us. He examined Jake from top to bottom. Tested his eyes, heart, took blood samples, the whole shooting match. He also mentioned one of the 'horrid things' that Vanessa had mentioned the night before – a brain tumour was a possibility, as walking into corners can be one of the symptoms.

Fortunately, our vets work with professionals and trainees from Nottingham University. The vet mentioned, that the only way to rule out the brain tumour, was with an MRI scan, and although they have a scanner at our vets, it's designed for horses, and therefore, may not be as accurate on small animals. He suggested that he speak to one of his colleagues at the University and discuss the best course of action. For now, he would prescribe some sedatives for Jake, which hopefully, should stop the fits. We would speak again when he had discussed things with his colleagues.

We returned home, and everyone was surprised to see Jake was with us. He had looked as bad as we thought, because Janet & Tracey both thought we might come back without him - that unbearable thought that had crossed our minds too...

Over coffee, we discussed with them what Luke had said, and after lots of cuddles – for both us and Jake – Janet, Tracey and the boys left to go home. Iain & I, both weary, decided to curl up with Jake and watch some TV. He slept for most of that day, bless him, he must have been so very tired, I know I was, and thankfully, just as the vet had said, he had no more fits.

On Monday morning, Jake was still bleary eyed, and not really interested in anything – except of course his breakfast. My theory was, that if he still had his appetite, things couldn't be too bad. Luke called to say that he'd spoken to a lecturer in veterinarian medicine from Nottingham University, and that he was happy to take a look at Jake.

However, we would need to take him to a veterinary hospital over towards Derby, which is around 40 miles away. He gave me the phone number, so I could call and make an appointment.

The young lady who answered the phone, was very sweet, and soon put my mind at ease. She gave me an appointment for the Friday morning, and said I could call any time if there were any problems. Much as I wanted to believe we could wait until then, it wasn't to be.

A few hours after the phone call, Jake almost went head first into his bowl of water and seemed to be very unsteady on his feet afterwards. Under different circumstances, I would have laughed at that, but not today…

I rang the Veterinary Hospital, again to tell them what had happened. The young receptionist said she'd see what she could do, and ring me back. Sure enough, within ten minutes, she was back on the phone, with an appointment for Wednesday, would that be okay?? You can bet your life it was! I called Iain to tell him, so that he could make arrangements at work to come with me.

We set off at 8-0 clock for the hospital. The weather was quite warm, but it was raining cats & dogs. How appropriate! It seemed to take forever to get there, but I guess in truth, it only took just over an hour. There's no quick way to get there, the route is mainly cross-country back roads. We took Spike along for the ride, we didn't know how long we would be, so didn't want to leave him alone for too long. Spike sat in the front with Iain, which he always liked, and Jake lay across my knee in the back. He had no enthusiasm for anything. Now and then, he'd lift his head and look at me, but mostly he slept. Thank God, he didn't know what awaited him.

The chap we met is a leading Veterinary Surgeon, who not only performs but teaches at the University. He's a very remarkable, amiable man, and he obviously loves both animals and his chosen profession. We filled him in on Jake's medical history, and then he asked us lots of questions. After our discussion, he examined Jake, and then explained the procedure. If it was, as he suspected, a brain tumour, then depending on where it was, it could be operable. He went on to clarify just what could – and couldn't be done. There was always the chance that things wouldn't go as expected, and we could possibly lose him during surgery. He went on to tell us that he believed the odds were slightly in Jakes' favour; but only just.

We could speculate all day, so the best thing to do, was to get the MRI done, and see what the results produced. In the meantime, he told us where we could get a decent cup of coffee, reassured us that Jake was in good hands, told us to try not to worry, and come back in an hour or so.

With the best of intentions, the vet asked us, if he found the tumour to be inoperable, should he just let him drift away? Without even thinking, I said 'Absolutely not!'

I'm sure there will be those who say that we should have said 'yes' to that question, but IF our little lad had to leave us, he would be in my arms, surrounded with love and people who knew him, and loved him. We couldn't contemplate just leaving him on an operating table.

I've said this to my son's so many times – if I knew where the 'mummy' button was, the one that controls the worrying etc. now might be a good time to turn it off! Alas, I have no concept of how to 'not worry' where my two legged or four legged boys are concerned!

We walked around the little town, until we found the coffee shop the vet had recommended. Neither of us could think of anything except our little lad. I said prayer after prayer, begging that Jake's life wouldn't end today, until finally, it was time to head back to the vets. The news confirmed pretty much what we'd expected – Jake had a brain tumour. There was however, a tiny little ray of hope when he said that he could operate. We didn't hesitate to say yes. It was agreed that they would keep him there and operate on him the following day. All being well, we would be able to bring him home in a few days' time.

We went home alone feeling somewhat apprehensive. Were we doing the right thing? They assured us he would only have the equivalent of a bad headache afterwards, and they would make sure he had pain medication. I found it hard to sleep that night, as did Iain, but there was nothing to be done now, except pray, hope and wait. He was in God's hands now...

We knew that we should prepare ourselves for the worst, but it was too painful to even try and envisage a life without Jake. I'm a firm believer in 'where there's life- there's hope!'

TICK...TICK...TICK...

We rang the surgery the minute we woke up. Jake was fine and was being prepped for surgery as we spoke. Call back after lunch. After lunch – there's no way either of us could eat a thing.

It's always the same isn't it; when you want the time to pass quickly, every minute feels like an hour. I managed to wait until twelve thirty, but I just had to phone. He was as well as could be expected, and the surgery had gone according to plan – no hiccups. I cried in relief. When I called later, he was awake, and having some food. That made me smile! He loves his chow! We would be able to collect him the following afternoon, but suggested we didn't visit him that night, as he needed to rest. That'll do for me!

Alas, that didn't last. He stopped eating, and didn't seem to want to drink either, so he had to stay there for a few more days, until they were satisfied he was sustained.

When he was finally allowed home, I asked a good friend to come along with me to collect him. I had known Mary for many years, and she loved animals as much as we do. When we arrived, we spoke to the vet, who assured us that everything had gone as well as they'd hoped, then he went off to get my little boy. Neither of us were quite prepared for the shock we had upon seeing him. His beautiful little face had been shaved, and now had a long stripe of staples down the middle of his snout. Oh, my poor, sweet boy, what have I done to you?

I was so happy to see him, but I just wanted to get him out of there and home where I could hug him to bits! Mary sat in the back with him and cuddled him all the way home. She has a very special gift of healing, and I know she was working on Jake all the way home. He slept most of the time and seemed quite confused when we got home. Spike was delighted to see him but went back to his bed after he'd had a good sniff.

That first night home was heart wrenching. He was crying out, but he didn't seem to want me to hold him. Could this be a side effect of his medication? The vet had promised me he wouldn't have too much pain. Eventually, I got a quilt, and lay down on the kitchen floor with him, as that's where he seemed to want to be. Spike joined us too – and then there were three! He kept getting in and out of his bed, but seemed unsure of what he wanted to do. I took him to the garden, and although he went out, he came straight back in again without cocking his leg. He squatted and wee'd in the conservatory which didn't matter to me, but he'd always been such a clean little fellow, it demonstrated that his mind was elsewhere.

I carried him up to our bedroom, where at least it was warmer. He didn't want to be on the bed, and finally settled in the corner, however, none of us got much sleep that night.

I don't know where to start about the events that followed...

Initially, Jake seemed to be alright, but very confused. We put that down to the operation and thought things would improve as time went on. We knew it would be a marathon and not a sprint. Slowly, he seemed to be getting his bearings back, but things were far from right. It was almost like he had to learn everything all over again! One incident that was particularly upsetting, was seeing him go to his water bowl and cry. He kept looking between me and the bowl, as if he didn't know what to do? When he went outside, it was like he was seeing everything for the first time.

The days passed rather slowly, and sadly, there didn't seem to be much improvement with him. We'd had him to the vets for a check-up, but there was nothing they could do. He had all the medication he needed. We had to give it time.

One day, he'd gone outside, but I couldn't see where he was. I found him head first, stuck behind the little ornamental well in the garden. He couldn't seem to reverse out, so between us, we had to pull him out. He seemed to be going backwards instead of forwards. After a few more days with no improvement, we spoke to our vet in Oakham, who said they would take him in for a few days to monitor his behaviour. I really did not want to leave him, but I knew 100% he was in the best possible hands. We spoke with the vets several times a day and went to see him the minute Iain got home from work. We took him for a walk in the little walking area, but he was still wanting to go around in circles…

After a week with them, he seemed to pick up a little, they removed all the staples, and suggested that he might be happier at home? You bet he would. I bundled him in the car before they changed their minds!

Things seemed to normalise for a little while, but progress was painfully slow. He was eating fine, liked to go out and do all the things he used to do, but he just wasn't my Jakey boy. It was very upsetting sometimes when I took him out. The odd, ignorant moron, would look at him as though he were some kind of freak, as the fur had not yet grown back on his face. It was reminiscent of the times some dim-wits thought we'd had his tail removed just so he could fight!!

One evening, he had another incident in the garden, only this time, he got himself stuck between the shed and the hedge. Iain had to take some of the fence to pieces in order to free him, he just couldn't or wouldn't move. This was ten steps backwards for me, and I had that gut wrenching feeling of Déjà vu.

Things went from bad to worse, and I knew it was only a matter of time – though I hoped with all my heart, it was just a little 'bump in the road.'

Sadly, after another traumatic incident we had to take him back to the vet. Again, he was admitted for observation, again, we worried ourselves senseless. We fell into the same procedure as before – phone calls every morning/visiting later, but I had a bad feeling this time, something was different.

Sure enough, a couple of days later, the vet called, and we had a long and lengthy discussion. It was time...

JAKES' LEGACY…

So, another August - another vets room. We sat on the floor with Jake, his little head resting on my leg. I gently stroked him and tried as best I could to soothe him. I don't even know if he knew I was there, but I prayed he recognised my voice. I gently stroked his beautifully soft, velvety ears one last time. It was so hard trying to speak calmly to him, when all I wanted to do was break down and cry. I told him that very soon, he would hear Daphne calling his name, and Mr. Wigs would be with her too!

She was coming to take him for the most wonderful walk to the most beautiful place, and they would have so much fun. Best of all, she would have his little tail with her, all fixed up and ready to wag!

I couldn't bring myself to sign the paper for Euthanasia; I left it to Iain. Memories of another painful August day danced around my mind. This is the worst kind of pain – one with no remedy. They say that time heals, but it doesn't – you cope and adapt. And anyone who tells me "it's only a dog" will get both barrels! I consoled myself with the thought that Mr. Wigs would be on hand to take him over 'The Bridge' and he'd be free of pain, just like that little pup he'd once been.

I thanked him for all the joy and happiness that he had brought to our lives, I told him how very much he was loved, and that we would love and miss him forever. We would NEVER, EVER forget him, and that one day, he'd be able to run and greet me once more.

Finally, I told him how very, very sorry we were because we'd had to let him go.... It was because we loved him, we had to let him go......I'd done all the deals with God; if you let him live, I promise I'll do this, that and the other. I would willing have given up some of my life to have him a little longer. It wasn't to be... We both lay on the floor and held our beautiful boy, as his little soul slipped away. He lay very peacefully, then it was all over.

I didn't want to let go of him. I wanted to bring him home and walk him in the woods; I wanted to chase him on the beach with a balloon; I wanted to blow raspberries on his tummy - I wanted him to live! I was seriously concerned that I was going to scream and wail, such was the feeling...

I kissed that beautiful, little face for the very last time and said goodbye.

There was absolutely no chance of hiding my tears, they were pouring down my face, along with that awful tightness in the throat when you can hardly breathe – I felt as if I was choking This overwhelming sadness and pain seemed to come from the depths of my soul. Heartbroken doesn't come anywhere near. Mummy's special little soldier was gone.

We drove home silently, except for my sobbing. I hurt so much I thought I wanted to die. Spike was waiting at the door when we arrived, I bent down to cuddle him and cried again. Normally, he wouldn't tolerate big cuddles, but that day, I was the first to move. He knew how sad I was, I hoped with all my heart he also knew why. Life was going to be very different from now on.

The next few days passed in a bit of a daze. I couldn't seem to get myself together, and cried many, many tears. The next hurdle came when the vet rang to tell us we could collect Jakes' ashes. It started all over again, the pain, the tears the heartbreak of losing him.

With loving care, I carried his ashes home, holding them as close to my heart as I possibly could. When we walked in, Spike eyed up the box I was carrying, so I put it down next to him, with the hope that somehow, he just might understand what had happened. He had a good sniff at it, then lay down beside it. I'm sure he knew.

For months, I took that little casket up to bed with me every night. Jake had always come up to bed with me for a snuggle, before going down to his own bed. I didn't see why this should change, Spike joined us in the bedroom too and slept in the corner where Jake had last been. I guess he was missing his buddy too.

It took an awful long time to come to terms with losing our boy, at times, it seemed like I would never be able to see a Red Staffy without bursting into tears. Even today, if I hear a song that reminds me of that time, I can't help but cry. Thankfully, we still had Spike – wonderful, crazy, not-wired-up-right Spike! Believe me, had it not been for him, things would have been much harder. It was almost like things had come full circle – we began with a Spike and are now left with a Spike.

Although, not in the best of health, and riddled with Arthritis, he plodded on, kept us on our toes, and still managed to make us laugh! He became very clingy after Jake had gone, understandable really. How on earth do you explain to a dog, that his best buddy's not coming home anymore? We tended to take him with us wherever we went, unlike Jake, he still loved going in the car, although we now had to help him in. Weather permitting, he would quite happily sit in the car whilst we did our shopping. He would have lived in there if we'd let him! We poured all our love into him and tried to ensure that however long we had left with him, we were going to make sure his every need was met, and he knew how very much was loved.

I'd like to share a quote with you that I recently read: -

"Every time I lose a dog, it's like they take a little piece of my heart with them. But every new dog that comes into my life, gifts me with a little piece of their heart. So, hopefully, if I live long enough, all the components of my heart will be dog, and I will become as loving, and generous as they are."

Wouldn't the world be a happier place?

I imagine Jake would have plenty to say about that...

ABOUT THE AUTHOR

Linda Meredith was born in the North West of England in Lancashire, but lived in Stalybridge, Cheshire, until at 19, she married an RAF serviceman, and moved away.

She has lived in several different places, both in the UK and abroad, and has had many different jobs from shop work, bank clerk to customer service manager – as well as being a full-time mum.

She now lives in the tiny, picturesque county of Rutland, where she has resided for 34 years, with her husband Iain, two dogs and one rabbit. A Staffy cross named Louie, and a full Staffy called Tia. The rabbit, known as Yabbit took up residence in their garden several years ago.

She and her husband have two sons, Terry and Christopher, who you will have met in this book. They both flew the nest many years ago, so their current babies are covered in fur, and have four legs.

Linda has always enjoyed reading and writing. She began by reading stories to her children, then graduated to writing and reciting poetry to anyone who'd listen!

Finally, after her beloved Jake passed away, she tried to write his story, but for many years, found it too painful to finish. After being inspired by reading **Sasha** and **Sheba – from hell to happiness** by the wonderful Brian L Porter, about the lives and his love for the dogs he rescues, she decided it was finally time to put Jakes story into words.

Fully Staffed is the emotional, moving, sometimes funny story of her love and devotion for the irreplaceable, crazy, dynamic duo, Jake and Spike...

—

.

Printed in Great
Britain
by Amazon